A Non-Violent
Revelation to John

A NON-VIOLENT REVELATION TO JOHN

Thomas Robert Jones

TRP

Tobacco River Publishers

A Non-Violent Revelation to John
Copyright © 1998 by Thomas Robert Jones

Library of Congress Cataloging-in-Publication Data

Jones, Thomas Robert.
    A non-violent revelation to John / Thomas Robert Jones.—1st ed.
      p. cm.
    Preassigned LCCN: 98-060518
    ISBN: 0-9664703-0-3

    1. Bible. N.T. Revelation—Drama. 2. Violence in the Bible. I. Title.

BS2825.5.J66 1998   228′.66
                                                QBI98-396

Library of Congress Card Catalog Number 98-060518

Printed in the United States of America
Design and composition by Sans Serif, Inc., Saline, Michigan

Published by

Tobacco River Publishers
11950 N. Meridian Road
Farwell, MI 48622

This Book is dedicated to

RUTH

For your love and patience

Acknowledgment

I want to thank everyone who read this manuscript and shared their suggestions and encouragement. I want to thank those people who bought copies pre-published and who gave me money to help pay for this book's publication. I want to thank students of Central Michigan University and the members of the summer bible study who have been so patient in helping me work this book out.

Contents

An Explanation of J.W. Bowman's Outline   viii

Preface   xi

The Theater and Cast   xx

Title   2

Salutation   4

Prologue   6

Act I   8

Act II   36

Act III   59

Act IV   78

Act V   99

Act VI   112

Act VII   133

Epilogue   144

Notes   147

An Explanation of J.W. Bowman's Outline

This explanation of "The Revelation to John" is presented as a Greek play. This idea was outlined by J.W. Bowman in his article "Revelation to John: Its Dramatic Structure," in the *Interpretation* Vol. IX, 1955, pages 436–453. J. W. Bowman was professor of New Testament Interpretation, San Francisco Theological Seminary, and has also published the Greek play outline in *The Interpreter's Dictionary of the Bible*, 1962.

The column of scripture printed on the outside margin of the pages of this book are the verses of scripture that compose the particular scene of the particular act referred to on those pages. For example, Act I, Scene I is from Rev. 2: 1–7. The verses Rev. 2: 1–7 are reprinted from the New Revised Standard Version of the bible in the outside margin, the text on the rest of the page is commentary on those verses.

"The Revelation to John" has in this Greek play version been divided into seven acts. Each act has a single setting, and within that setting occurs seven distinct scenes. In addition to the seven acts there is a title, salutation, prologue, epilogue, and closing benediction.

All scripture quotations are from the New Revised Standard Version of the Bible, copyright 1989 by the Division of Christian Education of the National Council of the Churches of Christ in the USA. All rights reserved. Used by permission.

I am greatly indebted to J. W. Bowman, for the insights of this book would have been impossible without using his Greek play outline of "The Revelation to John."

Here follows two paragraphs found on pages 439 and 440, Vol. IX, the *Interpretation*, 1955, of J. W. Bowman's explanation for his outline of John's Apocalypse.

"Accordingly, the thesis which we wish to defend in this article may be stated thus: first, the clue required for an adequate understanding of John's Apocalypse is to be found in its original design— that of a drama in seven acts, each of which in turn is composed of seven scenes; and secondly, only through grasping the nature of this dramatic structure of the book can its message be properly apprehended. A certain redundancy results from stating the article's thesis in this twofold manner: our wish is to stress the form of the book in the first item above and its content or message in the second, while at the same time suggesting that the two are inextricably combined and that it is due to a misunderstanding relative to the nature of the book's dramatic form that so many fantastic interpretations have been made of its teaching.

The Outline of the Revelation to John

It will be convenient at this point to present a new outline of the Apocalypse developed by the writer over a long span of years and to compare it with representative outlines proposed by others. In presenting this outline, the writer wishes it to be clear that he believes it to represent John's own way of conceiving of his book. John intentionally constructed it, in my judgment, on two literary models—first, as a drama of an original pattern (seven acts each consisting of seven scenes), but with certain features suggestive of the then-current Greek and Latin dramatic art with which his Christian readers in Asia Minor were familiar; and secondly, as a letter to the churches in that area, inasmuch as John could neither hope nor desire to see his drama enacted upon the stage of the Greek or Roman theatre."

J. W. Bowman's Outline of John's Apocalypse

Title 1: 1 – 3
Salutations 1: 4 – 6
Prologue 1: 7 – 8

<u>Act I   1: 9 – 3: 22</u>

Setting of Act I 1: 9 – 20

Scene 1, 2: 1 – 7
Scene 2, 2: 8 – 11
Scene 3, 2: 12 – 17
Scene 4, 2: 18 – 29
Scene 5, 3: 1 – 6
Scene 6, 3: 7 – 13
Scene 7, 3: 14 – 22

Act II   4: 1 – 8: 1

Setting of Act II   4: 1 – 5: 14

Scene 1, 6: 1 – 2
Scene 2, 6: 3 – 4
Scene 3, 6: 5 – 6
Scene 4, 6: 7 – 8
Scene 5, 6: 9 – 11
Scene 6, 6: 12: – 7: 17
Scene 7, 8: 1

Act III 8: 2 – 11: 18

Setting of Act III 8: 2 – 6

Scene 1,   8: 7
Scene 2,   8: 8 – 9
Scene 3,   8: 10 – 11
Scene 4,   8: 12 – 13
Scene 5,   9: 1 – 12
Scene 6,   9: 13 – 11: 14
Scene 7,   11:15 – 18

Act IV   11: 19 – 15: 4

Setting of Act IV   11: 19

Scene 1, 12: 1 – 17
Scene 2, 12: 18 – 13: 10
Scene 3, 13: 11 – 18
Scene 4, 14: 1 – 5
Scene 5, 14: 6 – 13
Scene 6, 14: 14 – 20
Scene 7, 15: 1 – 4

Act V   15: 5 – 16: 21

Setting for Act V 15: 5 – 16: 1

Scene 1, 16: 2
Scene 2, 16: 3
Scene 3, 16: 4 – 7
Scene 4, 16: 8 – 9
Scene 5, 16: 10 – 11
Scene 6, 16: 12 – 16
Scene 7, 16: 17 – 21

Act VI   17: 1 – 20: 3

Setting for Act VI 17: 1 – 2

Scene 1, 17: 3 – 5
Scene 2, 17: 6 – 18
Scene 3, 18: 1 – 19: 10
Scene 4, 19: 11 – 16
Scene 5, 19: 17 – 18
Scene 6, 19: 19 – 21
Scene 7, 20: 1 – 3

Act VII 20: 4 – 22: 5

Setting for Act VII 20: 4 – 10

Scene 1, 20: 11
Scene 2, 20: 12 – 15
Scene 3, 21: 1
Scene 4, 21: 2 – 8
Scene 5, 21: 9 – 21
Scene 6, 21: 22 – 27
Scene 7, 22: 1 – 5

Epilogue: 22: 6 – 20
Closing Benediction 22: 21

Preface

On The Nature Of God

God is love, and God will not do what is against God's nature to do.

Not all Christians believe this hypothesis. In his book on Revelation titled *Warning! Revelation is About to be Fulfilled*, Larry Wilson states:

> "A billion and a half casualties tell us that God is willing to sacrifice many for the salvation of others. After all, didn't He sacrifice His own Son for the salvation of all? We cannot conceptualize the breadth of God's interest in our salvation without considering the extensive destruction of the fourth seal. To some, this may sound terribly cruel and unfair. However, if the coming of Jesus is delayed another century, all 5.6 billion people currently living on earth would die anyway because the wages of sin is death. By accelerating the death of some people, others will be saved. This is a strange thing to say, but God is left—at times—with no other option but to destroy many to save a few. Remember the flood?"[1]

As we use the outline of the Greek play to study Revelation we will find that John is telling us something quite different than the perspective presented by Mr. Wilson. We will see the Nature of God as presented by the story of Jonah in the old Testament. Jonah heard the word of God and was told

> "Go at once to Nineveh, that great city, and cry out against it; for their wickedness has come up before me" (Jonah 1:2).

Jonah did not want to go, because Nineveh was an enemy of the Jews and extremely violent in war. After Jonah went his own way God returned him by a fish to land, and Jonah went to Nineveh and preached the most potent sermon ever delivered.

> "Forty days more, and Nineveh shall be overthrown!" (Jonah 3:4).

Then we are told the people of Nineveh

> "believed God; they proclaimed a fast, and everyone, great and small, put on sackcloth" including the king (Jonah 3:5).

---

[1]Wilson, Larry. *Warning! Revelation is About to be Fulfilled* (Brushton, NY: TEACH Services, Inc., 1984) p. 37.

Jonah had wanted the people of Nineveh to die. He wanted God to punish Nineveh, and when he saw that God was in the act of redeeming the city, Jonah became angry.

> "This was very displeasing to Jonah, and he became angry. He prayed to the Lord and said, 'O Lord! Is not this what I said while I was still in my own country? That is why I fled to Tar'shish at the beginning; for I knew that you are a gracious God and merciful, slow to anger, and abounding in steadfast love, and ready to relent from punishing" (Jonah 4:2).

The God of Jonah is the God that we see filled with compassion for the people of the Roman empire in the book of Revelation. When our hearts cry out for revenge, this God of Jonah reminds us that revenge is

> "sweet in the mouth but bitter in the stomach" (Rev. 10:10).

No matter what else is said or done in the Old Testament, it is the God of justice and love we hear proclaimed by Jonah that sits upon the great white throne of Revelation.

God is described as Love in the New Testament as well. We read in I John 4: 7–12:

> "Beloved, let us love one another, because love is from God: everyone who loves is born of God and knows God. Whoever does not love does not know God, for God is love. God's love was revealed among us in this way: God sent his only Son into the world so that we might live through him. In this is love, not that we loved God but that he loved us and sent his Son to be the atoning sacrifice for our sins. Beloved, since God loved us so much, we also ought to love one another. No one has ever seen God; if we love one another, God lives in us, and his love is perfected in us."

This God of love is the God of the Revelation, the same God who spoke to and through Jonah and is described in I John 4, as

> "Love." "In this is love, not that we loved God but that God first loved us and sent his Son to be the atoning sacrifice for our sins."

We are asked by some people to believe that God uses redemptive violence in Revelation and that this violence is directed against innocent people. I believe Revelation shows us that God will not do what is against God's nature to do. In the pages that follow I will show that the God in Revelation is Love.

Redemptive Violence

*The only redemptive violence used by God in Revelation is
against the Body of Christ!*

In stories of the Old West, bad guys take over the town. They steal
cattle, horses, and the monthly payroll. A stranger appears who is not
wearing a gun. He sees how terrible things are for the townspeople.
By persuasion, and with great reluctance, he takes up the gun. At
high noon the next day, he meets the bad guys in the middle of the
street and shoots them all. The stranger then rides out of town, with
the cheers and good wishes of the remaining townspeople at his
back.

This is a form of redemptive violence. A violent and evil deed is
committed to bring about a positive result. It is used by governments
against each other as well as against their own populations. Some
people believe "The Revelation to John" is about redemptive violence.
They interpret Revelation to mean that the world has become so evil
God comes and destroys the earth and its people, those who are
guilty and those who are innocent, in order to save the believers.

The Greek play format that J. W. Bowman says John used in writing Revelation makes clear that God does not come to destroy people
but rather to redeem them. Using Bowman's outline of "The Revelation" (Revelation has seven acts, and each act has a setting and seven
scenes, with a title, salutation, prologue, epilogue, and closing benediction), we will see that the violence usually attributed to God in Revelation does not happen, and in fact is replaced by acts of redemption.
Bowman discovered these divisions that allow the action of Revelation to stop at different places than it would using the biblical chapter
and verse.

Bowman's discovery allows us to see how the violent actions in
each act do not happen or how we are led to think they are sus-
pended until the following act. For example, in act two, scene six, we
would have thought the end of time had come if we had stopped reading with verse seventeen of chapter six. Using Bowman's Greek play
outline, we see that the end does not happen. Rather an angel ascending from the rising of the sun called with a loud voice to the four angels who had been given the power to damage earth and sea, saying,
"Do not damage the earth or the sea or the trees." This damage
never does take place in act two or any other act.

There *is redemptive violence* in Revelation. This redemptive violence, however, is always self-directed toward the Body of Christ:
sometimes it is the Body of Christ on the Cross and sometimes it is
the Body of Christ who are the believers. Christ takes the violence of

the world upon himself, and in Revelation we are told that as believers we may have to do the same.

On the Relationship of Christians and Jews

Jews are a part of the heavenly vision in Revelation as are Christians.
Jews do not have to become Christian in the Revelation
in order to be a part of that heavenly vision.

In writing Revelation, John is trying to bring the Jews and Christians together. Revelation was written at about the time the final split occurred between these two groups. Either that split had already happened and John was showing us in Revelation how such a split was contrary to the will of God, or he knew the split was about to happen and he was trying to prevent it from happening. John reminds the Christian believers that they are in this spiritual journey with the Jews, not separate from them. The entire context of his heavenly vision is drawn from the Jewish Bible, the Old Testament. He makes reference to the Old Testament over three hundred times in Revelation. John refers to the Old Testament to show that we can be Christian only within the context of the Jewish tradition. As we will see, John is telling us that the Jews have and will receive the salvation of God through practicing their Jewish faith, and will then share in the Heavenly Jerusalem with the Christians.

Confounding this view, some people have interpreted John's reference to the synagogues of Satan in Revelation as a condemnation of all Jews and their traditions, and thus a call to separate from them. It is important to understand the political context in which John speaks of the synogogues of Satan. John speaks specifically of synagogues in the cities of Smyrna and Philadelphia as the synagogues of Satan. At the time of John's letter, the Jews did not have to offer a pinch of incense to the Roman emperor as was required of Christians.

Vandenhoeck and Ruprecht give an explination of this pinch of incense in their book *Umwelt Des Neuen Testaments:*

"However, his son Domitian, who ruled at the end of the first century A.D., was of a different mind. He issued his instructions as divine commands by introducing official documents with the words 'Our lord and god commands that the following be done' (Suetonius Domitian XIII), and he required that everyone who spoke with him or wrote to him greet him with this reverential form of address. Anyone who resisted this felt the force of his wrath. Thus he had his kinsman the consul Flavius Clemens, put to death, and exiled Clemens' wife Domitilla for atheism. Their guilt apparently consisted in their having refused to recognize the emperor as god. Throughout the empire Domitian had imperial portraits set up, and in Ephesus he had a great temple built, with a larger-than-life-size statue of the emperor. This development is presupposed in the book of Revelation. While most of the inhabitants of Asia Minor were very willing to pay cultic reverence to the ruler because it was their custom to view him as a manifestation of the deity, for the Christians it was impossible to designate a man as lord and god. For them there was only one Lord of all Lords and only one King of all kings (Rev. 17:14; 19:16), who alone is to be venerated and worshiped.

"The cult of the emperor, which spread further and further in the Roman Empire, served primarily political aims; for the Romans did not prevent the many peoples who lived in the empire from worshiping their traditional gods, but, rather, granted them full freedom to practice the old traditional religions. The worship of the ruler was primarily a sign of political submission expressed in cultic form. Since the Jews were an ancient people with a venerable religion, they were not required to participate in the cult of the emperor. As a substitute, until the outbreak of the Jewish war, a daily sacrifice for the emperor was offered in the temple. Even after the Jewish war the rights that had been guaranteed to the Jews were maintained. At first the authorities in various places also counted the Christians as Jews or regarded them as a Jewish sect. But as soon as Jews and Christians became separate from each other, the Christians forfeited the privilege of sharing in the rights which the synagogue enjoyed. although the Christians acknowledged the authorities of the state as representatives of the order established by God, they could not possibly participate in a cultic veneration of the ruler."[2]

It is clear the Jews were exempt from being required to prove their political loyalty by venerating the Roman emperor because their faith would not allow calling any human being Lord. If the Jews would accept the Christians as a branch of Judaism, then the Christians would also be exempt from this law that required them to call the Roman emperor lord, and they would escape the death sentence that followed their refusal to offer incense to Caesar.

However, if the Jews and Christians were seen as one group it could cause difficulty for the Jews. The Jews may have been subject to the persecution and arrest suffered by the Christians in these cities if the Romans could not tell them apart.

From the *Anchor Dictionary of the Bible*, here is a description of the emperor Domitian and emperor worship.

"Domitian insisted on being recognized as a divine deus praesens, an important term in emperor worship (Cuss 1974: 139). Coins show him seated on a throne as 'father of the gods' (Abaecherli 1935), and a huge marble statue of himself in Ephesus became the focal point of the imperial cult throughout Asia Minor.

"Domitian insisted on being addressed, by letter or in person, as 'our lord and god' (Suet. Dom. 13; Scott 1936: 88–112) and all who refused were punished. That this persecution extended to Christians is clearly reflected in the

---

[2]*Umwelt Des Neuen Testaments*, trans. John E. Steely (Nashville: Abingdon Press, 1976) pp. 220–221.

book of Revelation (Scherrer 1984). Emperor deification, including offerings of incense, prayers, and vows, was now obligatory and used as a means to identify followers of the Christ. After his death in 96 C.E., statues of Domitian were destroyed by angry senators and he was declared 'an enemy of the state.' Many of his official decisions were rescinded by his successor, Nerva."[3]

The Jews in the cities of Smyrna and Philadelphia would not accept the Christians and may have been aggressive in denouncing them resulting in more frequent persecution for the Christians. We must not conclude that John is speaking about all synagogues or all Jews when he talks about the synagogues of Satan in Smyrna and Philadelphia. In the remainder of Revelation, John anchors the faith of the seven Christian Churches in the ancient faith of the Jews. He is being very specific in telling us here that the synagogues in Smyrna and Philadelphia, not all synagogues, were giving the Christians up to the authorities.

Satan, here and throughout the Revelation, most often refers to the Roman empire itself. We will lose the meaning of the Revelation if we create in our minds a creature called Satan that has any power at all, separate from human beings and the systems they create. The requirement that citizens of the Roman empire worship the emperor and proclaim him lord is the primary cause of the persecution of Christians. The synagogues of Smyrna and Philadelphia were aggressive in informing the Roman authorities that the Christians were not Jews. By so doing they played into the hands of the Roman empire, that is, Satan. The empire tried to force the Christians to offer the pinch of incense or suffer the consequences, so these Jews acted as agents of the Roman empire, thus agents of Satan. That is why these synagogues are called the synagogues of Satan.

Satan

Revelation has been misunderstood for centuries because we hold a non-Revelation understanding of Satan. I believe we will see that all satans, devils, beasts, and dragons in the Revelation are metaphors for human beings acting out the evil in their hearts.

Green slime, the possession of human bodies, heads that twist 360 degrees, unearthly sounds, and sinister strength are characteristics of Satan as depicted by Hollywood. In spite of how badly some people want this Hollywood Satan to be real, this creature of Hollywood

---

[3]*Anchor Dictionary of the Bible*, "Domitian" (New York: Doubleday, 1992), p. 807.

does not exist in "The Revelation to John." The Satan in Revelation is variously the systems established by emperors, dictators, presidents, generalissimos, first secretarys or any of their henchmen. John left it open to our imaginations to paint the portrait, for ourselves and for our time. In Revelation, Satan is the systems political leaders past or present have organized to do their will.

That the power of Satan is precarious and vulnerable is made clear in the Gospel of Mark.

> "And Jesus called them to him, and spoke to them in parables, 'How can Satan cast out Satan? If a kingdom is divided against itself, that kingdom cannot stand. And if a house is divided against itself, that house will not be able to stand. And if Satan has risen up against himself and is divided, he cannot stand, but his end has come. But no one can enter a strong man's house and plunder his property without first tying up the strong man; then indeed the house can be plundered" (Mark 3:23–27).

In this quote from Mark, Jesus has told us that no matter what form we give Satan, he is bound. The Satan in Revelation who is the empire has no power over people who refuse to give it power. All empires draw their strength from people's fear and willingness to give them power. It is clear from the evidence that the believers in the early church to whom John sent Revelation did not give up their power to the Roman empire Satan. They stood firmly and bravely, even unto death, as believers in the Lordship of Christ and the Kingdom of God. We will see in this interpretation of Revelation how this resistance has tied up Satan, "the strong man," and how these resisters speak Christ's words of redemption even to people who do evil.

Satan is and must be tied up. To believe in a Satan with power over us, power to make us do the will of Satan, is to believe in two gods. Jesus was asked,

> "Which commandment is the first of all?" He replied, "the first is, 'Hear O Israel; the Lord our God, the Lord is one'" Mark 12:29.

To understand Revelation and the redemptive love of God, it is critical to observe that we do not have:

A good god and a bad god
A big god and a small god
An old man god and a monster god
A heavenly god and an earthly god
A resurrected god and a fallen god

We have only one loving and redemptive God. No other entity or spirit has an indomitable power over us. We will see in "The Revelation to John" that no beast or dragon, devil or satan has an existence separate from the Roman emperor and his government. Revelation has been misunderstood for centuries because we have held a non-Revelation understanding of Satan.

God's Wrath

John shows the ultimate effect of God's wrath is not death, but rather redemption.

John teaches the reader of the Revelation that what humans feel and want and desire often is diametrically opposed to what God feels and wants and desires. Often John dupes us into learning the lessons he is teaching. He cons the reader into projecting onto the story feelings the reader is having, only to show how these same feelings, in reality, are contrary to the will of God.

The destruction of the Roman empire is one example. With the blowing of the seven trumpets, one-third of the world is going to be destroyed. Had we lived in the first hundred years after the resurrection, we would have thought of the earth as Asia, Africa and the Roman Empire. When we heard one-third of the earth would be burned up, if we were a persecuted Christian, we would be tempted to hope that the one-third being referred to is the empire. We would enjoy the thought of the Roman empire being destroyed. We are then told by an angel that our joy in the empire's death is a result of our misunderstanding the love of God. In the Revelation, God sends an angel to protect the Roman empire that God has not finished redeeming. Saying the empire is going to die may be "sweet in our mouth," but the reality of that destruction would be "bitter in our stomach."

There are several places John uses this technique of getting the reader to project their feelings onto the story, then showing the reader how they are wrong. We see this technique in the breaking of the sixth seal, the blowing of the first five trumpets, and especially when the two hundred million strong heavenly army comes to fight the Roman empire with the blowing of the sixth trumpet, and once more in the battle of Armageddon itself.

We are taught that human feelings of revenge and vengence are contrary to the will of God in John's writing about God's wrath. The meaning of the Greek word John uses for wrath is not clear. The New Jerusalem bible translates the word as anger, rather than wrath. It means an intense inner feeling welling up, and there is more than one choice. In several places in the Revelation I would choose passion (suffering), as it fits with the message of the Revelation, but I have stayed with wrath to be in harmony with the New Revisied Standard translation.

In chapter sixteen the angels pour out the seven bowls of the wrath of God. These bowls are not filled simply with God's wrath, rather they are filled with all that can be gathered of God's wrath. After these bowls are empty, "the wrath of God will be ended" Rev.15:1.

The first bowl brings foul and painful sores on those who worship the beast which is a metaphor for the Roman emperor. The second bowl killed all living things in the sea, thereby killing the evil in the sea. The third bowl turned the rivers and springs to blood. The fourth bowl allowed the sun to scorch the people who worshiped the beast, but those people lived through it and cursed the name of God. The fifth bowl plunged the Roman empire into darkness. The sixth bowl dried up the river Euphrates and allowed the kings of the east to come across. The seventh bowl proclaimed the great earthquake, a metaphor for the marching Roman army. This earthquake split the great city Jerusalem into three parts and destroyed the cities of the nations, yet we are not told that anyone dies. We are told that "they cursed God for the plague of the hail, so fearful was that plague" Rev.16:21. Out of all that is left of the wrath of God, the only death mentioned is the death of all that lives in the sea in order to kill the sea's evil.

These seven bowls of God's wrath in which no human is said to die amount to either not much wrath or not much of a God. The de-emphasis of death in these last seven plagues of the wrath of God is a writing technique. John is showing us that the expected violence of this wrath is a projection onto God's plan of our own desire for death and vengence. The ultimate effect of these bowls is not death, but redemption. We must not focus on death in these stories of the bowls, because it isn't there. John means for us to see that to the degree we feel God's wrath we are being warned to repent.

The Theater and Cast

The Theater: The Romans built many amphitheaters around the empire. Some of these held tens of thousands of people. Most were smaller. Our play takes place in an imaginary theater.

The Narrator: A Jewish Christian asks you, the reader, to go in your imagination to this play. This Jewish Christian gives you a narrative description of what is taking place. The theater has a stage, with seats forming a semicircle around the front of the stage.

The Characters: This play has a cast of hundreds of millions but from this incredible cast of humanity some characters will stand out more than others. The main characters will be the One, the Christ, Angels, and John the Seer of the vision, the Roman emperor (the First Beast), the emperor's priest (the Second Beast), and the Roman empire itself (the Great Red Dragon, or Satan).

The Audience: While much of the text in this book is a narrative description and explanation of the play as it unfolds you will discover that the audience plays an important role. Often during the play individuals in the audience will yell spontaneous responses toward the action on the stage. Individual people will also address the rest of the audience, or they will verbalize a prayer. The audience as a group has many responses to what is happening in the play. They cheer, applaud, whistle, hug, dance, slap each other on the back, kiss and hiss, cry, and hide their faces.

A Voice: This voice gives stage direction and description and is printed in italics.

Nero: Emperor of the Roman empire A.D. 54–68. Proclaimed himself a god and was accused of burning Rome; he used the Christians as scapegoats for the fire. He had the Christians of Rome killed with barbarous cruelty. It is thought that Peter and Paul both died in Nero's persecution of the Roman Christians. Nero was the emperor who started the siege of Jerusalem.

Vespasian: Emperor of the Roman empire A.D. 69–79. Was the general that led the siege of Jerusalem, leaving his son Titus to finish the job when Vespasian became emperor.

Domitian: Emperor of the Roman empire A.D. 81– 96. Proclaimed himself a god and instituted a reign of terror in his last years that included the Christians. Nero and Domitian are the models for the first beast of Revelation.

Trajan: Emperor of the Roman empire A.D. 98–117. Conquered Dacia and much of Parthia. Built much in Rome including the Forum of Trajan. Appointed Pliny the Younger as Proconsul-Priest of Bithynia-Pontus.

They Heard with Explanation

Standing before the Water Gate,
They wept,
Those people long ago.
Listening to Ezra
Reading,
Reading the law.

It had been lost
During their exile.
They had forgotten,
Or never knew.
Now they heard
With explanation.

Joy!
Tears of Joy!
Now they understood
God's love,
God's redeeming love!

Nehemiah 8:8 & 9

8:8 So they read from the book, from the law of God, with interpretation. They gave the sense, so that the people understood the reading.

8:9 And Nehemiah, who was the governor, and Ezra the priest and scribe, and the Levites who taught the people said to all the people, "This day is holy to the LORD your God; do not mourn or weep." For all the people wept when they heard the words of the law.

Title

Rev. 1:1–3

1:1 The revelation of Jesus Christ, which God gave him to show his servants what must soon take place; he made it known by sending his angel to his servant John,

1:2 who testified to the word of God and to the testimony of Jesus Christ, even to all that he saw.

1:3 Blessed is the one who reads aloud the words of the prophecy, and blessed are those who hear and who keep what is written in it; for the time is near.

The title verses of Revelation (Rev. 1: 1–3) were originally written on a separate piece of parchment and attached to the outside of the scroll that contained the rest of the play. Somewhere in time this "title" was incorporated as the first three verses of the book of Revelation.

The invitation to attend the play is extended to you, the reader, from a believer who is both Jewish and Christian. As the play proceeds, this person will be explaining to you the meaning of what is taking place. The performance takes place somewhere in Judea, about the year 90 A.D.

Use your imagination and let me guide you through this play. Let me describe to you what goes on. I will describe to you what happens on the stage, in the seven churches as their letters are read, and in the audience. The play is about the great tribulation we are going through, and what God intends to do about it. The title of the play is very long. It's called:

> "The revelation of Jesus Christ, which God gave him to show his servants what must soon take place; he made it known by sending his angel to his servant John, who testified to the word of God and to the testimony of Jesus Christ, even to all that he saw.
>
> Blessed is the one who reads aloud the words of the prophecy, and blessed are those who hear and who keep what is written in it; for the time is near."

This won't be like other Greek plays we have seen. John gets a special blessing for telling us this one, and we get a special blessing for hearing it. Did you catch the words in the title that said the time is near? That means it will be over soon for the Roman empire. That's what it's about, you know, the empire gets what it has coming! It's a prophecy about the end of evil, about the end of the Roman emperor, about the end of life on this earth as we know it, and about our new life in the kingdom of God. Come with me. It's going to tell us the answer to our question we pray every day,

"How long, O Lord, how long?"[1]

So use your imagination and come with me to the play. I must tell you that someone warned me about this play. They said it is full of surprises, and we should not get discouraged or give up. We have to wait to the end, to see how things really get worked out.

---

[1] Psalms 35:17–28

Salutation

Rev. 1:4–6

1:4 John to the seven churches that are in Asia: Grace to you and peace from him who is and who was and who is to come, and from the seven spirits who are before his throne,

1:5 and from Jesus Christ, the faithful witness, the firstborn of the dead, and the ruler of the kings of the earth. To him who loves us and freed us from our sins by his blood,

1:6 and made us to be a kingdom, priests serving his God and Father, to him be glory and dominion forever and ever. Amen.

The salutation (Rev.1:4–6) and benediction (Rev.22:21) put the play in the context of a personal letter from John, who has received it from an angel who has received it from Christ, who had received it from God. John then sends this letter to seven churches in Asia Minor.

Thank you, reader, for coming with me. Our imaginary theater is large. It was built by Herod the Great with the help of the emperor, to keep us happy with the empire. I bet those two had no idea a play that calls the emperor "beast" and his puppet king "the second beast" would be performed in their theater. Look over here, there is something posted on this wall. It's a salutation. This play is sent as a letter from John. Listen to what it says.

"John to the seven churches that are in Asia:
Grace to you and peace from him who is and who was and who is to come and from the seven spirits who are before his throne, and from Jesus Christ, the faithful witness, the first-born of the dead, and the ruler of the kings of the earth.
To him, who loves us and freed us from our sins by his blood, and made us to be a kingdom, priests serving his God and Father, to him be glory and dominion forever and ever. Amen."

Some of those churches in Asia Minor have it much worse than we do here in Judea. Since the Romans destroyed Jerusalem, they have left us alone, but the believers in Asia Minor face persecution every day.

Sometimes it feels like the empire is all there is in this world. It has lasted for so long, it has all power over us now, and it seems it will go on forever. But it is deceiving to think like that. God is still the greatest power in this world. God has been the greatest power since time began. No matter what the emperors say, or how much they make themselves out to be gods, they are nothing compared to Yahweh. Our

Lord the Christ is the One who is to come. Some say that evil fool Nero, the Roman emperor who tried but could not kill himself, is going to be resurrected and take the empire back, but we know Jesus is the One to come!

The salutation told us this play is from the seven spirits who are before the throne in heaven. Numbers are important. Seven means perfect. To say there are seven spirits means the Spirit of God is all there, it is complete, there is nothing lacking. And this play is from Jesus Christ, the faithful witness. That means faithful to the death. The death on the cross. So many believers have died since Christ died. They have been faithful witnesses too. The Romans say we are disloyal to the emperor because we will not call him "Lord." They kill us for treason. Jesus was the First, and he is our Lord.

He is the One who has come back from the dead, not Nero. He has come back from the dead and rules over the emperors, Nero included.

What love Jesus had for us all. To die like that. I think Jesus even loved the Romans, if you can believe it. He wanted to stop the violence, and he refused to do violence himself. He was like the lambs before slaughter who take on themselves the sins of the people. He is the lamb of God that takes away the sins of the world.[1] He wanted us to be a Kingdom of priests serving his God and Father. In former days only the Jews could be priests, but I think Jesus wanted the Christians to share the faith with the Jews. He wanted us all to be priests. Praise God we are able to see this play tonight. It is God and not the emperor or the Roman empire that has the true glory and control over the earth, now and forever!

Rev. 1:4–6

1:4 John to the seven churches that are in Asia: Grace to you and peace from him who is and who was and who is to come, and from the seven spirits who are before his throne,

1:5 and from Jesus Christ, the faithful witness, the firstborn of the dead, and the ruler of the kings of the earth. To him who loves us and freed us from our sins by his blood,

1:6 and made us to be a kingdom, priests serving his God and Father, to him be glory and dominion forever and ever. Amen.

-----
[1] John 1:29

Prologue

Rev. 1:7–8

1:7 Look! He is coming with the clouds; every eye will see him, even those who pierced him; and on his account all the tribes of the earth will wail. So it is to be. Amen.

1:8 "I am the Alpha and the Omega," says the Lord God, who is and who was and who is to come, the Almighty.

I was fortunate to find this seat. Everyone is talking. The stage is empty. We hear a voice as if from heaven,

> "Look! He is coming with the clouds;
> every eye will see him,
> even those who pierced him;
> and on his account all the tribes of the earth will wail.
> So it is to be. Amen."

It's like I told you, it is not emperor Nero that will come and take back the Roman empire. It is the Christ who will return on the clouds, and even the Romans will understand who he is. He is coming for all the earth. Not just the Jews, and not just the church, but he is coming to redeem all humans from the hand of evil. On that day the world will give up its pain. What a wail there will be on that great day.

The audience hears the voice again as if from heaven,

> "I am the Alpha and the Omega, says the Lord God, who is and who was and who is to come, the Almighty."

The audience begins to talk in whispers,

"Yahweh is the beginning and the end, Yahweh is the one who is and was and will come again. Yahweh has the power the Roman emperors claim for themselves. Yahweh is God Almighty our true Lord."

Act I

Rev. 1:9–3:22

Rev. 1:9–20

1:9 I, John, your brother who share with you in Jesus the persecution and the kingdom and the patient endurance, was on the island called Patmos because of the word of God and the testimony of Jesus.

The Setting

Each act begins with a section called the setting. In this section the stage is described and the backdrop developed for the act to follow. This will all make more sense if you remember to read from Revelation

Reader, are you still with me? I will try to explain everything as it takes place so you can understand clearly what is happening.

John appears and walks to the center of the stage.

"I, John, your brother who share with you in Jesus the persecution and the Kingdom and the patient endurance, was on the island called Patmos because of the word of God and the testimony of Jesus."

John is lucky that he was sent to Patmos. Most people in this audience have seen worse. Other Jews like John, who lived in this area, have been killed by the Romans or sent as war bounty to Rome, or as slaves to the mines, or to be eaten by dogs and wild animals in the hippodromes. They fought for the word of God, they tried to win their freedom from Rome, and Jerusalem was burned.

"Patient endurance," he says. Who can be patient when the Roman kingdom in which we live crushes us with oppression? Who can be patient when the Roman kingdom in which we live arrests the Christians like John our brother, and executes them as traitors to the emperor and the empire because they will not call Caesar "lord"?

The audience begins to chant,

"Thy Kingdom come, thy Kingdom come, thy kingdom come, thy kingdom come!" Someone yells, "Here and now!"

John continues,

> "I was in the spirit on the Lord's day, and I heard behind me a loud voice like a trumpet saying, 'Write in a book what you see and send it to the seven churches, to Ephesus, to Smyrna, to Pergamum, to Thyatira, to Sardis, to Philadelphia, and to Laodicea.'"

Most of us in the audience feel John deserved to be chosen for this task. He is a man of great spiritual strength. It is known that he prays, and thinks, and lives, in ways to reveal God's Kingdom. It was while he was in prayer on the Lord's day that he saw this vision. Christians have been worshiping on the first day of the week and call it the Lord's day.

John continues,

> "I turned to see whose voice it was that spoke to me, and on turning I saw seven golden lampstands, and in the midst of the lampstands I saw one like the Son of Man, clothed with a long robe and with a golden sash across his chest."

Reader, can you feel the power in this setting for the first act? On the stage we see the seven churches each represented by a lampstand. When we look at the churches we see the Son of Man. Christ should always be seen at the center of the churches. It takes courage for a church no matter how small or large to show Christ in their midst in the face of persecution. It takes vision on the part of the congregation to keep Christ as the center of the community. It takes forgiveness and the love of Christ, at the center of the church, to keep believers from becoming bitter and hateful toward the empire.

John says,

> "His head and his hair were white as white wool, white as snow; his eyes were like a flame of fire, his feet were like burnished bronze, refined as in a furnace, and his voice was like the sound of many waters. In his right hand he held seven stars, and from his mouth came a sharp, two-edged sword, and his face was like the sun shining with full force."

Rev. 1:10–15

1:10 I was in the spirit on the Lord's day, and I heard behind me a loud voice like a trumpet

1:11 saying, "Write in a book what you see and send it to the seven churches, to Ephesus, to Smyrna, to Pergamum, to Thyatira, to Sardis, to Philadelphia, and to Laodicea."

1:12 Then I turned to see whose voice it was that spoke to me, and on turning I saw seven golden lampstands,

1:13 and in the midst of the lampstands I saw one like the Son of Man, clothed with a long robe and with a golden sash across his chest.

1:14 His head and his hair were white as white wool, white as snow; his eyes were like a flame of fire,

1:15 his feet were like burnished bronze, refined as in a furnace, and his voice was like the sound of many waters.

Rev. 1:16–19

1:16 In his right hand he held seven stars, and from his mouth came a sharp, two-edged sword, and his face was like the sun shining with full force.

1:17 When I saw him, I fell at his feet as though dead. But he placed his right hand on me, saying, "Do not be afraid; I am the first and the last,

1:18 and the living one. I was dead, and see, I am alive forever and ever; and I have the keys of Death and of Hades.

1:19 Now write what you have seen, what is, and what is to take place after this.

My friend, this is the One described by Daniel.[1] Do you think this Son of Man will come to fight the Roman emperor, as the one in Daniel's vision came to fight the prince of Persia?

This Son of Man carries a different weapon then the One described in Daniel. From the mouth of this Son of Man comes a sharp, two-edged sword. The One the Jews have worshiped for so long now speaks through the voice of Christ. He speaks for the multitudes who are like many waters. He holds the leaders of the seven churches in his hand in the form of stars. Christ's concern for the church is more than a passing interest. Christ holds the church and its leaders in the very palm of his hand! The Light of Chrst reveals everything for his face is like the sun shining with full force.

On seeing this Son of Man shining like the sun the audience is on their feet cheering. The emperor Nero has tried to make us believe that he was the sun god, and had his image made like the sun. But Christ will outshine any emperor who has ever been, or is, or will be.

John holds up his arms for quiet.

"When I saw him, I fell at his feet as though dead. But he placed his right hand on me, saying, 'Do not be afraid; I am the first and the last, and the living one. I was dead, and see, I am alive forever and ever; and I have the keys of Death and of Hades.'"

The audience is again cheering.

We believe this is the Christ who has died and come back to life. There are many who want us to believe that it is the Roman emperor Nero who will come back to life. They are saying that Nero, that evil emperor, is going to come back to life and go to the east, to Persia, and raise a great army and recapture the empire. How we hate Nero. How we love the One Like the Son of Man. It is this One that holds the keys to both Death and Hades, and no emperor can come back from the dead without the Christ unlocking the door.

This One, like the Son of Man, is the first. It is this Son of Man who was present at the creation, and who talked with

---

[1] Daniel 10:6

Abraham and Moses. It is this Son of Man who is present with us and talks to us through John. It will be this Son of Man who will be present in the future, until the last scene of this play is finished.

John said the One like the Son of Man told him,

> "Write what you have seen, what is, and what is to take place after this. As for the mystery of the seven stars that you saw in my right hand, and the seven golden lampstands: the seven stars are the angels of the seven churches, and the seven lampstands are the seven churches."

Rev. 1:20

1:20 As for the mystery of the seven stars that you saw in my right hand, and the seven golden lampstands: the seven stars are the angels of the seven churches, and the seven lampstands are the seven churches.

Rev. 2:1–7

2:1 "To the angel of the church in Ephesus write: These are the words of him who holds the seven stars in his right hand, who walks among the seven golden lampstands:

2:2 "I know your works, your toil and your patient endurance. I know that you cannot tolerate evildoers; you have tested those who claim to be apostles but are not, and have found them to be false.

Scene I

"To the angel of the church in Ephesus write"

As the curtain opens on act one, the inside of a home in Ephesus is seen on the stage. A small group of Christians begins to assemble. It's about five o'clock in the morning and the angel (leader) of the church in Ephesus tells the group,

"We have to be more careful this morning, the Romans are out to get us again!"

There is excitement in her voice as she speaks in whispers to the group and tells them she has a letter from John, their brother in the faith who has been banished to Patmos. It is addressed to her as the leader of the church, and reminds them they are being held in the palm of Christ's hand, as Christ walks among the churches.

We listen to her read how Christ remembers their toil. These believers from Ephesus, like so many of us in the audience, will not join the artisan guilds because guild meals are held in pagan temples. The guilds take an animal to the temple to be sacrificed, and only a small portion is used for the sacifice so the rest is cooked for the guild meal. Meat sacrificed to idols, and fornication with humans or gods were the two practices most strongly condemned by our apostles at the Council of Jerusalem.[2] A Christian's faith keeps them out of the guilds, so they toil at hard labor and low paying jobs, like these Christians in Ephesus. Many in this church, as in most of the churches, are poor slaves. Their slavery and poverty, their meeting before dawn in secret and feeling like they are criminals to gather and pray, is beginning to take its toll on the group. How long will things go on like this? How long will they have to endure?

---

[2]Acts 15: 28–29

Their letter from John tells us that their pain comes from both inside and outside the church. They have had persons who claimed to be spiritual leaders or apostles, but who were not, come to them and want money, or tried to split up the church with teachings that would allow them to swear, "Caesar is Lord." Christ knows they have not accepted these imposters and they have spent the painful energy it takes to get free of them. Christ says it is to their credit that they have not allowed the mysterious Nicolaitans among them.

Because they shun the guilds and temple meals, as well as any form of emperor worship, they are poor and considered treasonous enemies of the Roman empire. For this, any of us in the audience, like the Christians in Ephesus, can be killed. If we are found guilty, we can be forced to lie on our backs with large stones put on our chests, and told we must "bear up." The stone and gravity will almost always win, resulting in our deaths. Nero dressed Christians in animal skins and gave them to the dogs. The emperor Nero used Christians as human torches to light his gardens for his parties at night.[3] This small church in Ephesus knows other Christians are suffering as they are suffering. Still they are complimented for "bearing up" under the rock of persecution, and for not growing weary.

A moan crescendoes from the audience when they hear the only criticism against the church in Ephesus.

"They had abandoned the love they had at first."

Rev. 2:3–4

2:3 I also know that you are enduring patiently and bearing up for the sake of my name, and that you have not grown weary.

2:4 But I have this against you, that you have abandoned the love you had at first.

---

[3] See note number one.

Rev. 2:5–7

2:5 Remember then from what you have fallen; repent, and do the works you did at first. If not, I will come to you and remove your lampstand from its place, unless you repent.

2:6 Yet this is to your credit: you hate the works of the Nicolaitans, which I also hate.

2:7 Let anyone who has an ear listen to what the Spirit is saying to the churches. To everyone who conquers, I will give permission to eat from the tree of life that is in the paradise of God.

This is the only fault the letter finds in them. We moan because these Christians live in a city with two temples for the worship of the Roman emperor. With two temples they will have twice as many celebrations where they must honor the emperor by calling him "Lord," or burn a pinch of incense as an offering. It is bad enough that most cities have one state temple. Having two will increase the severity of their persecution. They can't work at good-paying jobs because of the guilds. They know how Christians are persecuted and killed in the rest of the empire. They are not free to practice their faith openly. What group can keep the love they had at first under these circumstances? The audience feels angry, not loving, toward the empire. How can we keep the love we had at first as we watch loved ones put under the rock?

The audience hisses as someone shouts,

"Our God loves the Roman empire as much as our God loves us."

The hissing stops when the angel of the church in Ephesus reads,

> "Repent, and do the works you did at first. If not, I will come to you and remove your lampstand from its place, unless you repent."

We had heard this argument in our own church. When we see how bad things are, some of us want to stop loving our enemy. How can we find joy in spreading the Gospel after we see the price we must pay to do so? The promise from the letter to Ephesus says "those who conquer," and we all know that means "those who are martyred," will be given permission to eat from the tree of life in the paradise of God.

"Let anyone who has an ear listen to what the Spirit is saying to the churches."

Rev. 2:5–7

2:5 Remember then from what you have fallen; repent, and do the works you did at first. If not, I will come to you and remove your lampstand from its place, unless you repent.

2:6 Yet this is to your credit: you hate the works of the Nicolaitans, which I also hate.

2:7 Let anyone who has an ear listen to what the Spirit is saying to the churches. To everyone who conquers, I will give permission to eat from the tree of life that is in the paradise of God.

Rev. 2:8–11

2:8 "And to the angel of the church in Smyrna write: These are the words of the first and the last, who was dead and came to life:

2:9 "I know your affliction and your poverty, even though you are rich. I know the slander on the part of those who say that they are Jews and are not, but are a synagogue of Satan.

Scene 2

"To the angel of the church in Smyrna write"

The audience knows what the Christians of Smyrna face and there are murmurs of sympathy as the curtain goes up. Citizens of Smyrna are walking in a circle on the stage pointing to the small group of Christians from the church in Smyrna at the center of their circle.

We in the audience recognize those people doing the pointing. They are tax collectors, former Christians who have been forced to give up their faith, Roman soldiers, Jews, citizens of Smyrna who want to take the Christians' property, judges and jailers, and even brothers and sisters of the Christians. They are identifying the Christians, turning them in, to be tried for treason because they will not call Caesar "Lord."

This church more than others suffers persecution which can lead to death. In this letter Christ says through John,

"I am the First and the Last, the one who was dead and came back to life."

The church in Smyrna has to take comfort, as do we all, in knowing that the Christ does not call us to do what he will not do. Many of us in the audience will die for our faith, but he has died first, and he is the first to have been brought back to the life we will all share. The audience hears this as a word of hope, for we know we are being encouraged to be faithful unto death. We believe we will be given the crown of life.[4]

Christians of Smyrna are poor, even though they live in one of the richest cities in the empire. Like all Christians of the empire, they will not join the guilds because of the guilds' practice of eating meat offered to idols. Even though they can't work at jobs that earn them a livable wage and are therefore poor in material things, they are rich in faith.

---

[4] James 1:12

Christians and Jews alike understand that any testing or affliction caused by persecution is a benefit to faith. As their neighbors live in material wealth, the Christians in Smyrna live in spiritual wealth. This richness of faith is rewarded in this world and in the next. In this world we have community with each other. We know the Spirit of God is among us and we love and trust each other in the Spiritual Kingdom of which we are a part. The Christians in Smyrna are told not to fear what they are about to suffer, for in this world they have the comfort of knowing they will conquer and in the world to come they will receive the crown of life and escape the second death. The second death is the final fire.

The audience seems to be holding its breath when John, in the letter, talks about the synagogue of Satan.

This audience is filled with both Christians and Jews. Many people at this play are, like myself, both Christian and Jew, and we want to stay that way. Often the Romans can't tell us apart. Many synagogues allow Christians to worship with them. Most of us are of divided families, half Christians and half Jews. We both call the empire Satan and the emperor the Beast when we think we can get away with it.

Because Smyrna is a center of emperor worship, the people are required to burn incense and declare Caesar "Lord" more often than in most places. If the Jews of Smyrna are identified too closely with Christians, they will be forced to take part in this ritual that their faith can't allow. All of this could result in those Jews being persecuted like the Christians. They can lose their wealth and their life, so they disown the Christians. They point out the Christians to the authorities, who arrest them. The Roman empire's devil-slanderers who keep the prisons lock up the Christians, most for a short time and some forever. Most of us here know that Jews are betraying Christians in Smyrna and other places around the empire, and it causes bitterness between the Jews and Christians. The Christians believe these Jews are playing right into the hands of the empire. Since we call the Roman empire "Satan," we call the synagogues of these Jews "synagogues of Satan."

"Let anyone who has an ear listen to what the Spirit is saying to the churches."

Rev. 2:10–11

2:10 Do not fear what you are about to suffer. Beware, the devil is about to throw some of you into prison so that you may be tested, and for ten days you will have affliction. Be faithful until death, and I will give you the crown of life.

2:11 Let anyone who has an ear listen to what the Spirit is saying to the churches. Whoever conquers will not be harmed by the second death.

Rev. 2:12–17

2:12 "And to the angel of the church in Pergamum write: These are the words of him who has the sharp two-edged sword:

Scene 3

"To the angel of the church in Pergamum write"

There is a buzz in the theater as the audience discusses the third church which is at Pergamum. Many knew the Christian, Antipas, who was killed by the Romans in Pergamum. Some are angry, shouting for revenge, yelling that it is time for Christ to return with the heavenly army and wipe out the Romans. They think he should have done that the first time he was on the earth. The audience quiets as the curtain goes up on scene three.

Reader, can you see the church of Pergamum assembled on the stage? They are sharing a meal together as they wait for their letter to be read.

The angel of the church stands and begins the letter.

"These are the words of him who has the sharp two-edged sword."

The audience is excited and thinks the Christ will finally use the sword against the Romans. The sharp two-edged sword! With this weapon Christ makes war:

The angel reads from the letter,

"I will come to you soon and make war against them with the sword of my mouth."

Those in the audience who thought this was a sword of metal with which Christ will slay the Romans are disappointed. The sword coming out of Christ's mouth is a sword of words calling people to repentance and redemption. Do you remember how Christ called himself the bread of life[5] as a metaphor for being the daily lifegiver to the church? In this play Christ is using the sword as a metaphor for the spoken word of God.

Most of us who are Christians in the audience believe nonviolence is the teaching of Christ. No Christian will

---

[5] John 6:35

serve in the army of the empire. The only violence we can take part in results in Christians, as the body of Christ, taking the violence upon ourselves. Most of us have no trouble understanding Christ's reference to the sword as a metaphor. We can't conceive of our Christ, who lived among us and told us to love even our enemies, using an actual sword.

People in the audience begin to shout sayings of Christ about swords.

"I have not come to bring peace, but a sword."[6]

We all know what sword that saying is about. The sword of the Romans against the faithful! We, Christians, as the body of Christ, stop violence by taking the violence upon ourselves.

Someone else yells the words of Christ,

"Put your sword back, it is not the way, for all who take the sword will perish by the sword."[7]

A woman stood and reminded the audience that Jesus told his disciples,

"Two swords are enough."[8]

Someone in the audience yells out,

"How can two swords be enough against an empire?"

We know that for someone who taught nonviolence two swords would be too many. In the teachings of Christ, the Spiritual Kingdom is a nonviolent Kingdom, except when we Christians, as the body of Christ, take the violence of the world upon ourselves.

Christ tells the church in Pergamum through their letter,

"I know where you are living, where Satan's throne is."

Rev. 2:12

2:12 "And to the angel of the church in Pergamum write: These are the words of him who has the sharp two-edged sword:

---

[6] Matthew10:34
[7] Matthew 26:52
[8] Luke 22:38

Rev. 2:13–16

2:13 "I know where you are living, where Satan's throne is. Yet you are holding fast to my name, and you did not deny your faith in me even in the days of Antipas my witness, my faithful one, who was killed among you, where Satan lives.

2:14 But I have a few things against you: you have some there who hold to the teaching of Balaam, who taught Balak to put a stumbling block before the people of Israel, so that they would eat food sacrificed to idols and practice fornication.

2:15 So you also have some who hold to the teaching of the Nicolaitans.

2:16 Repent then. If not, I will come to you soon and make war against them with the sword of my mouth.

Pergamum is the greatest center of emperor worship in Asia Minor, as well as having temples to Athena and Zeus on their sacred hill. It is no wonder Christians in Pergamum suffer persecution the way they do. They have far more people to betray them than the rest of us. In addition, their Roman governor has the right of the sword—the right to kill the Christians who will not call Caesar Lord. He is the proconsul for most of Asia Minor. His is the throne of Satan, the throne of the empire, the throne of death!

The angel of the church in Pergamum continues to read.

"Yet you are holding fast to my name, and you did not deny your faith in me even in the days of Antipas my witness, my faithful one, who was killed among you, where Satan lives."

The audience stands and applauds the brave souls of Pergamum, who have not called Caesar lord.
Christ does have this against them:

". . . you have some there who hold to the teaching of Balaam, who taught Balak to put a stumbling block before the people of Israel, so that they would eat food sacrificed to idols and practice fornication. So you also have some who hold to the teaching of the Nicolaitans."

Most of us know very little about the Nicolaitans. Some think the Nicolaitans and the teachers of Balaam might be the same people. Balaam is that Old Testament gentile prophet the rabbis have taught us to think badly of. Whoever the Nicolaitans are, they eat food sacrificed to idols and practice fornication. The Nicolaitans teach it is all right for Christians to join the guilds in order to make a good living. They say there is nothing wrong with eating the guild meals, which contains meat offered to idols. But if we do that, we will be fornicating with idols.

The angel continues to read,

"Repent then. If not, I will come to you soon and make war against them with the sword of my mouth."

Those of us in the audience know the call to repent is not just for that small group of Christians from Pergamum on the stage. That call comes to all of us, to repent from creating idols and calling someone "Lord" who is not Lord. When we hear the words,

"I will come soon and make war against them with the sword of my mouth,"

someone from the audience calls out,

"Come, Lord Jesus!"

The angel from the church in Pergamum reads to the audience,

"I will give a white stone, and on the white stone is written a new name that no one knows except the one who receives it."

Those who conquer, who are martyred, will receive a white stone from Christ. A white stone is the ticket that got us into this play; perhaps now it will get us into the Kingdom of God. A white stone means an accused is found not guilty by a jury. Perhaps with this white stone we will be found not guilty and invited into the Spiritual Kingdom of God. Sometimes we put a white stone in a bag around our neck with a secret name on it. It gives us power because only we know the meaning of the name.

The angel reads these words of Christ,

"To everyone who conquers I will give some of the hidden manna."

Christ is our bread of life! He used bread to say he was the daily life-giver to the church as the manna gave daily life to the Israelites in the wilderness so long ago. Tradition has taught us that the only manna to survive into the promised land was put into an urn and kept in the temple as a reminder of the forty years the Jews had wandered in the wilderness. Our Jewish tradition teaches us that Jeremiah hid this manna in a cave before the temple was destroyed the first time and that the Messiah would return this hidden manna to the people. In this letter to Pergamum, Christ says he will give some of this hidden manna to everyone who conquers. To conquer as Christ did is to die for one's faith. If we are to receive this Jewish manna, how then can we divide the tradition of the Jews and the faith of the Christians. We are one!

"Let anyone who has an ear listen to what the Spirit is saying to the churches."

Rev. 2:17

2:17 Let anyone who has an ear listen to what the Spirit is saying to the churches. To everyone who conquers I will give some of the hidden manna, and I will give a white stone, and on the white stone is written a new name that no one knows except the one who receives it.

Rev. 2:18–29

2:18 "And to the angel of the church in Thyatira write: These are the words of the Son of God, who has eyes like a flame of fire, and whose feet are like burnished bronze:

2:19 "I know your works —your love, faith, service, and patient endurance. I know that your last works are greater than the first.

Scene 4

"To the angel of the church in Thyatira write"

I am not sure exactly how to describe it to you, but there is something different about this church as the curtain opens on the fourth scene. The people are sitting scattered around the stage, some with their backs to each other.

The angel [leader] of the congregation in Thyatira stands to read them their letter from John.

We can hear from the tone of this letter that the church in Thyatira is in more trouble than the last three churches because

"The Son of God who has eyes like a flame of fire, and feet like burnished bronze"[9]

is watching. The audience finds this picture of the Son of God, from the letter, frightening. Here is the very Son of God, whoes eyes reflect the furnace which held Shadrach, Meshach, and Abednego—the Son of God who was the first of those to be raised from the dead, and who walks with feet more powerful than those of the Romans. We understand these people have to change something about their church, immediately!

The letter goes on,

"I know your works—your love, faith, service, and patient endurance. I know that your last works are greater than the first."

There is confusion in the audience. We know about this church. They have a reputation of working hard to live the gospel. Their love is real, and the help they give each other and strangers is well known. Their acts of kindness to other churches are amazing. As their angel reads them their letter, we hear the Son of God has this against them:

---

[9] Daniel 10:6

"You tolerate that woman, Jezebel,[10] who calls herself a prophet and is teaching and beguiling my servants to practice fornication and to eat food sacrificed to idols."

Someone in the audience yells,

"Women can't be prophets! Next they'll want to be apostles!"

A woman answers,

"It's not that she is a woman prophet. The problem is what she teaches her followers!"

An argument breaks out between the women and the men.

The same woman is now addressing the audience.

"There are women apostles traveling from church to church evangelizing. Haven't they been to your churches?"

"Women are apostles and prophets and teachers in our churches. You must know of Phoebe, the diakonos of the church in Cenchreae. Not only is she the minister, but they have also made her Bishop!"[11]

She continues to speak.

"Who has not heard of Prisca, who worked with Paul in Christ Jesus and risked her neck for Paul's life? We are all in debt to Prisca who, along with her husband Aquila, moved because of persecution, from Rome to Corinth and from Corinth they went to Ephesus with Paul. We have heard of the churches she started in her home. We know it was Prisca who explained the way of God more perfectly to Apollos, who then became a co-worker with Paul. Prisca was a great teacher in those churches she started, and many of us believe Prisca wrote the letter to the Hebrews.[12]

"And you know of Junia, she was a believer before Paul, and has spent time in prison. Paul calls her an apostle, and we know there is no higher office!"[13]

Rev. 2:20

2:20 But I have this against you: you tolerate that woman Jezebel, who calls herself a prophet and is teaching and beguiling my servants to practice fornication and to eat food sacrificed to idols.

---

[10] I Kings 16:31
[11] Romans 16:1
[12] Romans 16:3–4
[13] Romans 16:7

Rev. 2:21–23

2:21 I gave her time to repent, but she refuses to repent of her fornication.

2:22 Beware, I am throwing her on a bed, and those who commit adultery with her I am throwing into great distress, unless they repent of her doings;

2:23 and I will strike her children dead. And all the churches will know that I am the one who searches minds and hearts, and I will give to each of you as your works deserve.

The same woman continues,

"And what of Lydia?[14] She was the first convert in Philippi. After her conversion, she and her household were baptized, and they became a church in her home. Who does not believe that she was the leader in that church?"

The audience is respectful as the woman continues,

"Paul called Euodia and Syntyche[15] his coworkers. He said these two women struggled beside him in the work of the gospel, along with Clement and the rest of his coworkers, whose names are in the Book of Life. Do you think these women just served tea? They took the risk with Paul and the rest of the coworkers of being killed for spreading the gospel. They were apostles who traveled around spreading the Word.

"Some of us know the four daughters of Philip,[16] great women prophets who have visited our church. We still talk about the Eucharist they led while they were there, and many of us still pray the prayers they taught us in our private worship."[17]

After a pause, the woman sits down and the angel from the church in Thyatira continues with the letter.

"I gave Jezebel time to repent, but she refuses to repent of her fornication. Beware, I am throwing her on a bed, and those who commit adultery with her I am throwing into great distress, unless they repent of her doings; and I will strike her children dead."

Someone from the audience asks,

"What is she doing wrong?"

A man answers,

"She teaches that we can join the guilds and make lots of money. She says it does not hurt to eat the meat that has been sacrificed to idols, and if forced, we can proclaim Caesar is lord. These are the fornications she is committing. We all know if we worship idols it kills the spirit, so we may as well be dead!"

---

[14] Acts 16:14

[15] Philippians 4:2

[16] Acts 21:8

[17] Notes 3–8 from *Women of Spirit: Female Leadership in the Jewish and Christian Traditions*, Rosemary Ruether, Eleanor McLaughlin (New York: Simon and Schuster, 1979) pps. 30–39.

The letter continues,

"And all the churches will know that I am the one who searches minds and hearts, and I will give to each of you as your works deserve."

The Jews in the audience nod in agreement, for they know that keeping the law is their means of salvation, and they believe that the way we live makes a difference in our relationship with God.

More of the letter is read,

"But to the rest of you in Thyatira, who do not hold this teaching, who have not learned what some call 'the deep things of Satan,' to you I say, I do not lay on you any other burden; only hold fast to what you have until I come."

Someone yells out,

"Gnostics, there are gnostics in Thyatira! Gnostics say they know the deep things of God but we know their knowledge only helps the empire, so we call their knowledge the knowledge of the deep things of Satan."

The angel finishes reading the letter,

"To everyone who conquers and continues to do my works to the end, I will give authority over the nations; to rule them with an iron rod, as when clay pots are shattered—even as I also received authority from my Father."

A man wanting vengeance yells out,

"What a great day that will be! We can't wait for the day we can bust the Romans in the head with a rod of iron!"

Christ says in the letter,

"To the one who conquers I will also give the morning star."

So, do you understand, reader, who it is who conquers? Those who conquer are the ones who do not give in, the ones who do not take on the enemy's face and commit violence but who take the violence upon themselves. These are the ones who will be given the morning star, the very Spirit of Christ himself!

"Let anyone who has an ear listen to what the Spirit is saying to the churches."

2:24 But to the rest of you in Thyatira, who do not hold this teaching, who have not learned what some call 'the deep things of Satan,' to you I say, I do not lay on you any other burden;

2:25 only hold fast to what you have until I come.

2:26 To everyone who conquers and continues to do my works to the end, I will give authority over the nations;

2:27 to rule them with an iron rod, as when clay pots are shattered —

2:28 even as I also received authority from my Father. To the one who conquers I will also give the morning star.

2:29 Let anyone who has an ear listen to what the Spirit is saying to the churches.

Rev. 3:1–6

3:1 "And to the angel of the church in Sardis write: These are the words of him who has the seven spirits of God and the seven stars: "I know your works; you have a name of being alive, but you are dead.

Scene 5

"To the angel of the church in Sardis write"

The people from Sardis wander onto the stage talking to each other. Their leader finally gets their attention and starts to read.

"These are the words of Him who has the seven spirits of God and the seven stars: I know your works; you have a name of being alive, but you are dead."

Our Lord, Jesus, has the seven spirits of God, the complete spirit of God and knows the spirit of each of the churches' leaders. For as we saw in the setting of this act, the One who is the First and the Last holds the seven stars in his hand.

Sardis has no temples dedicated to the emperor. Because they do not have a temple in which to worship the emperor in the city of Sardis, the Church in Sardis does not suffer much persecution. The Christians get along with the Jews in Sardis, because if the Christians are not being persecuted, the Jews are not in danger by being associated with them, therefore there is no cause for confrontation.

Sardis has it easy compared to Pergamum. In Pergamum they are always on the watch. Antipas was killed in Pergamum for his faith, and Christians of Pergamum are sent to Rome for martyrdom if they are Roman citizens. This persecution of Christians is not consistent but is more or less severe at different times. Unlike Sardis, Christians in the church at Pergamum, as well as Thyatira, Ephesus and Smyrna, are threatened with death every day, yet they are alive through their faith.

Reader, can you see that these Christians on the stage from Sardis are alive, yet the threat of death from persecution is not real to them? That is why John writes to them, "but you are dead." Their faith has lost its power and life for they do not need faith to give them daily strength. They do not share the suffering that this audience knows to be real.

The Christians of Sardis feel they do not need the Spirit of God to give them strength to keep faithful, courage to spread the gospel, desire to meet for worship even if it means arrest. Most of us in this audience believe, if we do not suffer persecution or share in the persecution and pain of other churches,

"we are dead."

The angel of Sardis reads from the letter,

"Wake up, and strengthen what remains and is on the point of death, for I have not found your works perfect in the sight of my God."

When they hear, "Wake up," the Christians from Sardis start to pay attention. Their city had been captured by foreign armies twice in their history when the sentries fell asleep, so they have a reputation of being sleepy people.

The letter continues,

"Remember then what you received and heard; obey it and repent. If you do not wake up, I will come like a thief, and you will not know at what hour I will come to you."

Jesus is warning them he will be like the armies that climbed their cliff and scaled their wall while they slept. He will come while they are not paying attention and when he is least expected.

Some in the audience laugh at the Christians of Sardis because of their chastisement. We all know we have to hear the warning which comes to them. We must join in the suffering if we are going to be the church. We can't let people suffer from the violence of the empire without suffering with them. We can't exploit others as the rich exploit us. We know we are called to be Christians of peace, spreading peace to all people.

Again the angel reads,

"Yet you have still a few persons in Sardis who have not soiled their clothes; they will walk with me, dressed in white, for they are worthy."

Rev. 3:2–4

3:2 Wake up, and strengthen what remains and is on the point of death, for I have not found your works perfect in the sight of my God.

3:3 Remember then what you received and heard; obey it, and repent. If you do not wake up, I will come like a thief, and you will not know at what hour I will come to you.

3:4 Yet you have still a few persons in Sardis who have not soiled their clothes; they will walk with me, dressed in white, for they are worthy.

Rev. 3:5–6

3:5 If you conquer, you will be clothed like them in white robes, and I will not blot your name out of the book of life; I will confess your name before my Father and before his angels.

3:6 Let anyone who has an ear listen to what the Spirit is saying to the churches.

There are always the faithful in every church and synagogue—a few men, but most of them are old women. Old women stay faithful no matter what the rest of the group does.

John writes in their letter,

> "If you conquer, you will be clothed like them in white robes, and I will not blot your name out of the book of life; I will confess your name before my Father and before his angels."

All of our towns in Judea have a register with the names of every citizen. When Christians are arrested and killed, their names are removed from the book. But we will be given the white robes of martyrdom and our names will never be removed from the book that God keeps. If we conquer, if we hold fast to our faith and don't give in to the empire even if it means death, Jesus will confess our name before all who are in heaven.

> "Let anyone who has an ear listen to what the Spirit is saying to the churches."

Scene 6

"To the angel of the church in Philadelphia write:"

As this sixth scene begins, a small group of Jews are standing on the steps of their synagogue, confronting some Christians who want to enter.

In the city of Philadelphia, as we saw was true in the city of Smyrna, the local synagogue has closed its door to the Christians. These synagogues are called the synagogues of Satan. Remember, the Jews do not have to burn incense to the emperor; they pay a tax instead. In Philadelphia and Smyrna the Jews are telling the authorities that Christians are not Jews. As a result, the Christians suffer persecution or death as traitors because they will not burn the incense. In our lives, Satan is the Roman empire. When the Jews in Philadelphia turn the Christians over to the authorities, they are playing into the hands of the empire, so they are called the synagogues of the Satan-empire. Not all synagogues are synagogues of Satan, only those who turn in the Christians.

Their letter says,

> "I will make those of the synagogue of Satan who say that they are Jews and are not, but are lying—I will make them come and bow down before your feet, and they will learn that I have loved you."

The audience knows the Old Testament scripture that says the gentiles will bow down to the feet of the Jews.[18] Now it will be reversed. God is going to prove to the Jews that Christians share in the special calling and love of God.

Since the synagogue has closed its door to the Christians, Christ, the Holy One, the True One, who has the key of David, opens a new door on the stage.[19] The first door allowed safe entrance into the synagogue for the Christians of Asia Minor. The second door allows them entrance into the

---

[18] Isaiah 60:14
[19] John 10: 9

Rev. 3:7–13

3:7 "And to the angel of the church in Philadelphia write: These are the words of the holy one, the true one, who has the key of David, who opens and no one will shut, who shuts and no one opens:

3:8 "I know your works. Look, I have set before you an open door, which no one is able to shut. I know that you have but little power, and yet you have kept my word and have not denied my name.

3:9 I will make those of the synagogue of Satan who say that they are Jews and are not, but are lying—I will make them come and bow down before your feet, and they will learn that I have loved you.

Rev. 3:10–13

3:10 Because you have kept my word of patient endurance, I will keep you from the hour of trial that is coming on the whole world to test the inhabitants of the earth.

3:11 I am coming soon; hold fast to what you have, so that no one may seize your crown.

3:12 If you conquer, I will make you a pillar in the temple of my God; you will never go out of it. I will write on you the name of my God, and the name of the city of my God, the new Jerusalem that comes down from my God out of heaven, and my own new name.

3:13 Let anyone who has an ear listen to what the Spirit is saying to the churches.

Spiritual Kingdom of God. We are all invited to pass through.

In this Kingdom we must never stop loving, even our enemy, whoever our enemy may be. This Spiritual Kingdom is founded in our Jewish faith. Jews and Christians will learn to share this Kingdom together. In this Kingdom there is no room for violence. Do you remember that in Scene Three Christ has redefined making war with the sword to making war with the sword of his mouth. Women share the most important leadership roles with men in this Kingdom. The prophet of the congregation in Thyatira is a woman. The problem, in Thyatira, was not that a woman was prophet, but what she was teaching as prophet. We never walk alone in the Kingdom, for we all share in the world's joy and pain. If prosperity, then we share with others. If pain or persecution, then we all share in the pain or persecution. In the previous scene, the church in Sardis is told they are dead because they do not share in the struggle of the other churches.

A man yells out,

"Not on your life! Love everyone, even my enemy? No! Share the faith with Jews? No! Give up defending myself with force for the way of Christ? No! Share leadership with women? No! Share with the poor? No!"

Then a meek voice from the audience says,

"I want to love everyone, but I'm afraid. I have nothing against Jews, but didn't they kill our Lord? I know we have to stop violence, but how will we protect ourselves? I think women should be equal, but I'm happy our church doesn't have a woman leader. I know I should do something for the poor, but it's not my fault they're poor. I will share more but first I need to get my affairs in order."

We all go through the open door into the Spiritual Kingdom by the grace of God. We go through with our prejudices, our fears, our weaknesses, our hesitancies, but all those who enter this Spiritual Kingdom will inherit the New Jerusalem.

Their letter continues,

"If you conquer, I will make you a pillar in the temple of my God; you will never go out of it. I will write on you the name of my God, and the name of the city of my God, the new Jerusalem that comes down from my God out of heaven, and my own new name."

Even with their shortcomings and their sins, with their lack of power, the Christians in Philadelphia have kept Christ's word and have not denied Christ's name.

The letter reads,

"Because you have kept my word of patient endurance, I will keep you from the hour of trial that is coming on the whole world to test the inhabitants of the earth. I am coming soon; hold fast to what you have, so that no one may seize your crown."

Someone asks,

"What is he talking about, the hour of trial that is coming on the whole world? Are things going to get worse?"

"Let anyone who has an ear listen to what the Spirit is saying to the churches."

Rev. 3:14–22

3:14 "And to the angel of the church in Laodicea write: The words of the Amen, the faithful and true witness, the origin of God's creation:

3:15 "I know your works; you are neither cold nor hot. I wish that you were either cold or hot.

3:16 So, because you are lukewarm, and neither cold nor hot, I am about to spit you out of my mouth.

Scene 7

"To the angel of the church in Laodicea write"

Do you like this play so far? In this last scene of the first act there are people dressed in beautiful wool capes with silk and jewels filling up the stage.

The audience whispers to each other,

"These can't be Christians!"

The angel of the church in Laodicea raises his hand and says

"These are the words of the Amen."

We use the word amen to swear that what we are about to say is true. John is telling us in this letter, Christ is the Amen, Christ is the Truth. Christ is the Faithful and True Witness, the One who has gone to the cross. Christ is the Origin of God's Creation. Not a part of, or just a witness to the creation, but the Origin of the Creation, and that is the truth.

"He was in the beginning with God. All things came into being through him, and without him not one thing came into being."[20]

We know Laodicea is a city of great wealth, a trade center. They have a medical school that makes medicine for both ears and eyes. Laodicea prospers. It is so rich, when the earthquake destroyed it, the citizens of Laodicea rebuilt the town from their own money with no help from the emperor. They told the emperor,

"We are rich, we have prospered, and we have need of nothing."

Not just the town but the Church in Laodicea is rich. Someone in the audience yells out,

"A church cannot be a church if it is rich!"

---

[20] John. 2-3

Their leader reads on,

"You say, 'I am rich, I have prospered, and I need nothng.' You do not realize that you are wretched, pitiable, poor, blind, and naked."

The Christians from Laodicea who are on the stage look very uncomfortable. Christ in the letter tells them to buy gold from him which has been refined by fire,[21] then they will truly be rich. That is to say, the gold of experience, that has seen and suffered the persecution and pain of the other churches of Asia Minor.

Money has become their God in Laodicea.[22] They put their trust and their security in money. They provide their food with money, they chose their friends by how much money they have. They think they have happiness and well-being only if they have money. They do not look to God for their security. As a result Jesus says to them in this letter,

"I know your works; you are neither cold nor hot. I wish that you were either cold or hot. So, because you are lukewarm, and neither cold nor hot, I am about to spit you out of my mouth."

The people on the stage begin to squirm. The letter tells them if they buy this gold that has been refined by fire, they will receive white robes to clothe them and to keep the shame of their nakedness from being seen, and salve to anoint their eyes so that they may see.

Those of us in the audience understand that as rich and fine as their clothing is, they can't rely on the beautiful cloth made from the wool of Laodicea. They must be willing to take on the white robe of persecution, given by Christ. If they use only the salve produced at the medical school of Laodicea, they will be blind to those sights of the soul that lead to life. They need to reach out for that salve of faith that gives us spiritual sight.[23]

Are we deaf? Do we use the powder made in Laodicea for our ears?[24] We also need to listen with our soul, for as the

---

[21] Isaiah 1:25–26
[22] Mark 10:25
[23] Mark 10:46
[24] Mark 7:32

Rev. 3:17–19

3:17 For you say, 'I am rich, I have prospered, and I need nothing.' You do not realize that you are wretched, pitiable, poor, blind, and naked.

3:18 Therefore I counsel you to buy from me gold refined by fire so that you may be rich; and white robes to clothe you and to keep the shame of your nakedness from being seen; and salve to anoint your eyes so that you may see.

3:19 I reprove and discipline those whom I love. Be earnest, therefore, and repent.

Rev. 3:20–22

3:20 Listen! I am standing at the door, knocking; if you hear my voice and open the door, I will come in to you and eat with you, and you with me.

3:21 To the one who conquers I will give a place with me on my throne, just as I myself conquered and sat down with my Father on his throne.

3:22 Let anyone who has an ear listen to what the Spirit is saying to the churches."

letter says, Christ is standing at the door knocking. If we hear his voice and open the door, he will come in to us and eat with us and we with him. We can keep our faith hot to the boiling point by dealing with the issue of money without fear, and motivated by love.

They finish reading the letter. Those who conquer are those who are willing to die as Christ has died.

"I reprove and discipline those whom I love. Be earnest, therefore, and repent . . . To the one who conquers I will give a place with me on my throne, just as I myself conquered and sat down with my Father on his throne.

"Let anyone who has an ear listen to what the Spirit is saying to the churches."

Here Ends the First Act

The One

The One
Was seated on the throne.
The One who looked like Jasper.
A bow of green,
Emerald green
Arched above the One.

It was a cow that started the song.
A heavenly song.
The cow with many eyes,
And wings, six wings.

It was the cow that started to sing.
Then the lion with many eyes,
The flying eagle spread its wings,
And the human face joined in,
Around the Color on the throne.

Blinding Light, made rumbling thunder,
Shaking the glassy sea.
Shaking twenty-four crowns of gold.
Crowns lying before the One,
Thrown by twenty-four elders.
Toward the Color, the Light, the One.

The One,
Not man,
Not woman,
The One is Other.
The One is Light.
The One is Color.
Holy, Holy, Holy, is the One.

Rev. Chapter 4:3–8

4:3 And the one seated there looks like jasper and carnelian, and around the throne is a rainbow that looks like an emerald.

4:4 Around the throne are twenty-four thrones, and seated on the thrones are twenty-four elders, dressed in white robes, with golden crowns on their heads.

4:5 Coming from the throne are flashes of lightning, and rumblings and peals of thunder, and in front of the throne burn seven flaming torches, which are the seven spirits of God;

4:6 and in front of the throne there is something like a sea of glass, like crystal. Around the throne, and on each side of the throne, are four living creatures, full of eyes in front and behind:

4:7 the first living creature like a lion, the second living creature like an ox, the third living creature with a face like a human face, and the fourth living creature like a flying eagle.

4:8 And the four living creatures, each of them with six wings, are full of eyes all around and inside. Day and night without ceasing they sing, Holy, holy, holy, the Lord God the Almighty, who was and is and is to come."

Act II

Rev. 4:1–8:1

Rev. 4:1–5:14

4:1 After this I looked, and there in heaven a door stood open! And the first voice, which I had heard speaking to me like a trumpet, said, "Come up here, and I will show you what must take place after this."

4:2 At once I was in the spirit, and there in heaven stood a throne, with one seated on the throne!

4:3 And the one seated there looks like jasper and carnelian, and around the throne is a rainbow that looks like an emerald.

4:4 Around the throne are twenty-four thrones, and seated on the thrones are twenty-four elders, dressed in white robes, with golden crowns on their heads.

The Setting

A blinding streak of light streams through an open door hanging above the dark stage. The voice of the One, like the Son of Man, who had sounded like a trumpet in the first act, is calling to John and saying,

"Come up here, and I will show you what must take place after this."

John is transported in the spirit through that door and into the heavenly presence.

We are stunned at the beauty of the heavenly space. There is the very throne of the One, and

"seated on that throne is One that looked like jasper and carnelian, and around the throne is a rainbow that looks like an emerald."

This is the Creator God that the Jews have followed for so long.[1] They know it is wrong to make an image of this God, for the One is not a creature that can be sculpted out of rock or drawn in the sand. The One is not male, not female, the One is Other, the One is Light, the One is Color. Around the One is the rainbow to remind us that our God is not a God of destruction and death, but of creation and life.[2] If Jesus takes us into the presence of this Jewish God, why are there so many people trying to separate the Christians and the Jews? We must stay together or Christians like myself and those in this audience will die. We must accept each other and help each other bear up the rock of the empire's oppression, for it is the One that has blessed us both.

---

[1] Exodus 20:4
[2] Genesis 9:15

36

We can see that the Christians and Jews get along in heaven and share the heavenly presence, for around the throne of the One are the thrones of the twelve Christian apostles and twelve elders of the tribes of Israel. These twenty-four elders have shared the empire's life of oppression and death common to us all, for they wear the white of martyrs. But theirs is the victory, for on their heads are golden crowns.

The audience cowers at the flashes of lightning, and rumblings and peals of thunder that come from the throne and roll across the theater. Someone calls out,

"What are those seven torches, around the throne?"

Those are the seven torches which are the Spirit of God, the whole, complete, all-seeing, and all-knowing Spirit of God. Look, there is a new kind of sea in the heavenly presence. A sea of glass with the twenty-four thrones around it, a sea that looks like crystal, a sea that can be used to watch the earth.

"Around the throne, and on each side of the throne, are four living creatures, full of eyes in front and behind: the first living creature like a lion, the second living creature like an ox, the third living creature with a face like a human face, and the fourth living creature like a flying eagle."

Do you think these are the living creatures of the prophet Ezekiel, that great old prophet of the Jews, who saw them in a vision?[3] Christians can't be separated from those old visions. Christians can't be separated from our tradition which has been given us from our Jewish brothers and sisters. Christians can't be separated from the Jews, who have been given the promise of the One to be the chosen people.[4] These living creatures have six wings and are full of eyes in front and behind so nothing goes unobserved by heaven. These are the four living creatures that lead the worship in the heavenly space.

---

[3] Ezekiel 1:5ff
[4] Genesis 12:3

Rev. 4: 5–8

4:5 Coming from the throne are flashes of lightning, and rumblings and peals of thunder, and in front of the throne burn seven flaming torches, which are the seven spirits of God;

4:6 and in front of the throne there is something like a sea of glass, like crystal. Around the throne, and on each side of the throne, are four living creatures, full of eyes in front and behind:

4:7 the first living creature like a lion, the second living creature like an ox, the third living creature with a face like a human face, and the fourth living creature like a flying eagle.

4:8 And the four living creatures, each of them with six wings, are full of eyes all around and inside. Day and night without ceasing they sing, Holy, holy, holy, the Lord God the Almighty, who was and is and is to come."

Rev. 4:9–5:2

4:9 And whenever the living creatures give glory and honor and thanks to the one who is seated on the throne, who lives forever and ever,

4:10 the twenty-four elders fall before the one who is seated on the throne and worship the one who lives forever and ever; they cast their crowns before the throne, singing,

4:11 "You are worthy, our Lord and God, to receive glory and honor and power, for you created all things, and by your will they existed and were created."

5:1 Then I saw in the right hand of the one seated on the throne a scroll written on the inside and on the back, sealed with seven seals;

5:2 and I saw a mighty angel proclaiming with a loud voice, "Who is worthy to open the scroll and break its seals?"

The human leads the worship and sings,

"Holy, holy, holy, the Lord God the Almighty, who was and is and is to come."

The lion leads the worship and sings,

"Holy, holy, holy, the Lord God the Almighty, who was and is and is to come."

The eagle leads the worship and sings,

"Holy, holy, holy, the Lord God the Almighty, who was and is and is to come."

The cow leads the worship and sings,

"Holy, holy, holy, the Lord God the Almighty, who was and is and is to come."

The audience is on their feet cheering, laughing and pointing when the cow leads the worship, but they stop when the twenty-four elders,

"fell before the One who is seated on the throne and worshiped the One who lives forever and ever."

The One has no competition in heaven. No one, not even the twenty-four elders, tries to play God, or usurp God's power, for they know that the One is just and loving in all things. When the twenty-four elders fall before the One,

"they cast their crowns before the throne, singing, 'You are worthy, our Lord and God, to receive glory and honor and power, for you created all things, and by your will they existed and were created.'"

The One has a scroll,

"written on the inside and on the back, sealed with seven seals."

This is like the scrolls we use when we sell a piece of land in Israel. At the year of Jubilee, a relative of the person who sold the land can ask for the scroll, break the seals, and get the land back without payment.[5] We never actually sell the

---

[5] Leviticus 25:8–17

land for the land belongs to the One. We only lease the land until the year of Jubilee.

A mighty angel proclaims with a voice so loud it could be heard in heaven and on earth and by the dead under the earth,

"Who is worthy to open the scroll and break its seals?"

The audience is not clear about what has been sold, and what will be given back. Then we watch as the stage fills with creatures of all creation. Birds, animals of the forest, animals of the plains, wild animals and domesticated animals, fish and all manner of creatures from the sea, snakes and lizards and insects, bugs that fly and crawl and hop, clean and unclean animals together fill the stage. Creation is what has been sold. The creation had been given to Adam and Eve to nurture them and give them life, and because of their sin they lost it.[6] Now Creation is in the hands of evil men and women who destroy the earth, who kill God's creatures with cruelty, and who murder God's people with oppression and slavery.

As the play continues, John says,

"No one in heaven or on earth or under the earth was able to open the scroll or to look into it. And I began to weep bitterly because no one was found worthy to open the scroll or to look into it."

We weep with John. We long to find someone who can restore the Garden. We have been waiting for the One who can bring the Kingdom of God upon the earth. We pray for the One who can stop the greed and violence and war that has caused so much suffering and death among us. If no one can be found to open the scroll, the creation will stay in the hands of violent humans. Someone must be found to break the seals! It's not going to take just any relative of Adam and Eve to redeem the lost garden, and it's not going to take just money to buy back the creation. It is going to take someone who has not been contaminated by the violence and hatred of this world—someone not filled with violence, war and sin to restore the garden. If no next of kin can be found, then the land stays in the hands of the oppressors. The earth will be

Rev. 5:3–5

5:3 And no one in heaven or on earth or under the earth was able to open the scroll or to look into it.

5:4 And I began to weep bitterly because no one was found worthy to open the scroll or to look into it.

5:5 Then one of the elders said to me, "Do not weep. See, the Lion of the tribe of Judah, the Root of David, has conquered, so that he can open the scroll and its seven seals."

---

[6] Genesis 2:18–3:24

Rev. 5:6–10

5:6 Then I saw between the throne and the four living creatures and among the elders a Lamb standing as if it had been slaughtered, having seven horns and seven eyes, which are the seven spirits of God sent out into all the earth.

5:7 He went and took the scroll from the right hand of the one who was seated on the throne.

5:8 When he had taken the scroll, the four living creatures and the twenty-four elders fell before the Lamb, each holding a harp and golden bowls full of incense, which are the prayers of the saints.

5:9 They sing a new song: "You are worthy to take the scroll and to open its seals, for you were slaughtered and by your blood you ransomed for God saints from every tribe and language and people and nation;

5:10 you have made them to be a kingdom and priests serving our God, and they will reign on earth."

lost forever to the rule of madness and war. That is why John weeps. That is why we weep with him.

"Then one of the elders said to John,

"Do not weep. See, the Lion of the tribe of Judah, the Root of David,[7] has conquered, so that he can open the scroll and its seven seals."

A sigh sweeps the audience, as they hear that someone can bring about salvation for all Creation. When the elder explained that the Lion of the tribe of Judah and the Root of David can open the scroll, it became clear that our salvation will come from the Jews. Someone who has inherited the blessing of David the King[8] will be found to open the scroll. As Christ has redefined making war, so Christ has turned the Lion of the tribe of Judah into a Lamb. See the Lamb standing on the stage, standing between the throne and the four living ceatures and among the elders. This is no ordinary lamb for this Lamb has already been slaughtered. We know the Lamb is perfect because its horns and eyes are of the perfect and complete number. The Lamb has seven horns, which we know to mean it has all power. The Lamb has seven eyes which are the seven Spirits of God, the complete Spirit, who is sent out into all the earth with the ablility to see all and know all.

The Lamb that has been slaughtered,

"went and took the scroll from the right hand of the One who was seated on the throne."

He is the One who has conquered over death, and is Worthy. Worthy because he has not participated in the world's violence, but rather has taken the violence of the world upon himself. It is Christ who has won the right to open the scroll and bring the Kingdom into being.

When the Lamb took the scroll, the twelve apostles and the twelve elders of Israel, along with the four living creatures,

[7] Genesis 49:8–9 Isaiah 11:1–9
[8] 2 Samuel 7:10–17

"fell before the Lamb, each holding a harp and golden bowls full of incense, which are the prayers of the saints. They sang a new song:

'You are worthy[9] to take the scroll
and to open its seals,
for you were slaughtered and by
your blood you ransomed for God
saints from every tribe and language and people and nation;
you have made them to be a kingdom and priests serving our God
and they will reign on earth.'"

It was by taking the violence of the world on himself, and not responding in kind, that the Lamb can redeem the earth and restore the Kingdom. Now it is not just the Jews who will serve as priests to our God, but the Jews and Christians together have been made into

"a kingdom of priests serving our God, and they will reign on earth."

Singing with full voice are

"many angels surrounding the throne and the living creatures and the elders; they numbered myriads of myriads and thousands of thousands."

With incredible beauty they sing,

"Worthy is the Lamb that was slaughtered
to receive power and wealth and wisdom and might
and honor and glory and blessing!"

These angels are then joined by all God's creatures that have been waiting on the stage, birds and animals, fish, snakes and lizards, and insects, and all there is on the earth, and in the sea, and they sing,

"To the One seated on the throne and to the Lamb
be blessing and honor and glory and might
forever and ever!"
"And the four living creatures said, 'Amen!' And the elders fell down and worshipped."

---

[9] Mark 15:21–41

Rev. 5:11–14

5:11 Then I looked, and I heard the voice of many angels surrounding the throne and the living creatures and the elders; they numbered myriads of myriads and thousands of thousands,

5:12 singing with full voice, "Worthy is the Lamb that was slaughtered to receive power and wealth and wisdom and might and honor and glory and blessing!"

5:13 Then I heard every creature in heaven and on earth and under the earth and in the sea, and all that is in them, singing, "To the one seated on the throne and to the Lamb be blessing and honor and glory and might forever and ever!"

5:14 And the four living creatures said, "Amen!" And the elders fell down and worshiped.

Rev. 6:1–2

6:1 Then I saw the Lamb open one of the seven seals, and I heard one of the four living creatures call out, as with a voice of thunder, "Come!"

6:2 I looked, and there was a white horse! Its rider had a bow; a crown was given to him, and he came out conquering and to conquer.

Scene 1

Every eye is on the heavenly stage as the Lamb steps forward to open the first seal. As the seal is broken one of the four living creatures calls out with a voice of thunder,

"Come!"

From the side of the stage comes a white horse.

"Its rider had a bow; a crown was given to him, and he came out conquering and to conquer."

This is a beautiful sight, for the rider's bow is brilliantly translucent. It seems to create its own light, and the theater is awash in its many colors. The audience starts to cheer and shout when the colors from the rainbow strike them. This is the bow the One had given Noah.[10] It was taken from the sky and is now carried by the rider of the white horse. The bow has always reminded us our God is not a God of destruction and death, but our God is a God of creation and life. Who is this on the white horse? Is this the One in human form? Is this the Lamb himself? Is this the Spirit of God that goes out over the face of the whole earth?

The rider says nothing as he accepts the crown. This is a crown of victory, and the audience is on their feet cheering their new king. What joy we feel to know there will be victory over the death and slavery of this world. There will be victory over death itself, and the One in the heavenly space will be our king. We all remembered the price that the Lamb has paid for this victory, the price of the cross, and we are humbled into silence.

Do you remember, the setting for this act has shown us that the natural order will be redeemed by the Lamb. Things will go back to the way they were in the Garden before war and violence and death came upon the earth. Here on the stage we see that garden, before there was time, before there was history, before there was memory. The One

---

[10] The word used here as "bow" can have the same meaning as the bow of the clouds found in Genesis 9: 8–17.

has come conquering and to conquer. The One has conquered nothingness with creation. The One has conquered the heavens by creating the sun by day and the moon by night.[11] The One has conquered silence by creating the land and sea and all their creatures. The One has conquered loneliness by creating humans in the image of God. Into this garden comes the white horse and its rider, but the rider is not finished with conquering. The One knows that violence and death will invade the garden, so the One has given the crown of victory to the rider who will conquer violence and death by redeeming them on the cross![12] This victory will be greater than has been won by any of the Roman armies, or any armies that have come before them since the time of Nimrod.[13] This victory will be greater than any army will achieve in all the time yet to come. The victory of this King on the white horse is the victory over death, the victory over the human will to revenge and to retaliate. It will be a victory over all violence by not returning violence for violence.[14]

Rev. 6:1–2

6:1 Then I saw the Lamb open one of the seven seals, and I heard one of the four living creatures call out, as with a voice of thunder, "Come!"

6:2 I looked, and there was a white horse! Its rider had a bow; a crown was given to him, and he came out conquering and to conquer.

---

[11] Genesis 1:14–19
[12] Romans 6:1–14
[13] Genesis 10:8–11
[14] 1 Corinthians 1:18–31

Rev. 6:3–4

6:3 When he opened the second seal, I heard the second living creature call out, "Come!"

6:4 And out came another horse, bright red; its rider was permitted to take peace from the earth, so that people would slaughter one another; and he was given a great sword.

Scene 2

Christ the Lamb steps to the front of the heavenly stage and opens the second seal. As he does, the second living creature calls out,

"Come!"
    "And out came another horse, bright red; its rider was permitted to take peace from the earth, so that people would slaughter one another; and he was given a great sword."

Many in the audience hug their knees, hiding their faces from this red horse and its rider. We know this horse. It has traveled through our land from the time of Nineveh, from the days of Cain. Its color is not red. This horse has another color that you cannot see. It has been through so many battles, so many sieges, it has stepped on the bodies of so many humans, it has been swimming in so much blood, its color has been lost, and now it wears the color of its crimes.

This is the horse that brought destruction to the Holy City and murdered hundreds of thousands of Jews. This horse has conquered many lands for the Roman empire, and many lands for empires past, and will conquer many lands for empires yet to come. How beautiful the Garden before this rider on the red horse is given the sword. It gives us pain to know that the sword has been given. How wonderful life would have been if this rider and his red horse had never entered the Garden at all. Some blame the One for giving the sword to the rider of the red horse. Others said it is we humans who give the sword.

One of the women in the audience shouts,

"God allowed Cain to kill his brother Abel,[15] but God did not tell Cain to kill him. God allowed humans to corrupt the earth and to fill it with violence before the flood,[16] but God did not want the violence and corruption. God allowed Nimrod to become the first mighty warrior and to build Nineveh,[17] a city filled with war, but God did not tell Nimrod to do this. God does not force us to love. It is not God that gives the sword, we are the sword-givers!"

---

[15] Genesis 4:3–9
[16] Genesis 6:1–8
[17] Genesis 10:8–11

She continues,

"We can work in the trades for good money, making the shields and swords and spears and armor that destroy us. We can feed the army and help build their war machines. Our boys can be taken into Roman armies for the purpose of killing. We can pay homage and send taxes to the madness of the emperor, who can wipe out an entire people with one word as though he were God. We allow war and the making of war to consume like a ravenous monster both our wealth and our people. It is all of us here, all who witness this play, who give the rider of the red horse the sword and allow him to take peace from the earth."

A man yells out,

"How can we stop this rider on the red horse? How can we go up against so great an enemy?"

The woman yelled back,

"Have we forgotten the words of our Lord? I say to you, love your enemies and pray for those who persecute you, so that you may be children of your Father in heaven."[18]

The man responds,

"Loving our enemies will not win wars. Loving our enemies will not make them stop harassing and oppressing. Loving our enemies will not protect our property or our rights or our lives."

The woman answers,

"What loving our enemies will do, is make us children of the One who is in heaven! Our love will become power, and God will use this power to redeem our enemies! That is what loving our enemies will do. That is enough. We will not be children of a nation, country, or empire, but of the Kingdom of God. In the Kingdom there can be no violence if the Kingdom is to be real! We must stop giving the rider on the red horse permission to take peace from the earth! We must be willing to take the violence of war and the violence of the empire upon ourselves, just as Christ took the violence of the empire's cross upon himself!"

---

[18] Matthew 5:44–45

Rev. 6:3–4

6:3 When he opened the second seal, I heard the second living creature call out, "Come!"

6:4 And out came another horse, bright red; its rider was permitted to take peace from the earth, so that people would slaughter one another; and he was given a great sword.

Rev. 6:5–6

6:5 When he opened the third seal, I heard the third living creature call out, "Come!" I looked, and there was a black horse! Its rider held a pair of scales in his hand,

6:6 and I heard what seemed to be a voice in the midst of the four living creatures saying, "A quart of wheat for a day's pay, and three quarts of barley for a day's pay, but do not damage the olive oil and the wine!"

Scene 3

We know what will happen now. The Lamb is going to walk to the front of the stage and open the third seal. When he does, the third living creature will call out with a voice of thunder,

"Come!"

The people who are in the theater are not sure we want the third seal to be opened. It is enough that violence has invaded the Garden. It is enough that the One has to conquer by sending the Lamb to the cross. It is enough that we are told if violence is to be redeemed, we will need to follow the example of the Lamb and take the blows of the empire upon ourselves. It is more than enough that we are not to lose the love we had at first, and love even the empire! What will happen now in this play of surprises and reversed expectations?

When the third living creature calls out, "Come!" there appears a

"black horse! Its rider held a pair of scales in his hand, and I heard what seemed to be a voice in the midst of the four living creatures, calling out, 'a quart of wheat for a day's pay, and three quarts of barley for a day's pay, but do not damage the olive oil and the wine!'"

We know this black horse well, for it lives in our stomachs. It pushes against the walls of our children's stomachs until they are distorted and huge. It causes the children's legs to bend in and their knees to knock together. It causes their eyes to glaze over and stare into a world we cannot see. The black horse of hunger has always followed the red horse of war. Hunger is part of war and violence. Starvation can't be stopped when all the food has gone to feed the army.

Starvation can't be stopped when the fields have been burned by the Romans to starve us out and make us surrender. It is the children who surrender first, even if the adults keep fighting. The children are always the first to become sick and malnourished; they are always the first to die.

How we hate this black horse and its rider! Our anger turns to rage when we are reminded of the edict of the emperor Domitian.[19] There was not enough beer in Rome so he ordered the vineyards and olive groves of this part of the empire cut back so more grain could be raised to produce more beer. Then even more of our grain would be sent to Rome to keep the Romans from rioting for lack of bread and beer! But what about us? What about our children? What about our old ones? We starve in order to keep Rome alive. It takes a day's pay now to buy one quart of wheat or three quarts of barley. The rider of the black horse carries a set of scales. It's more than wheat or barley that is measured on those scales; it is also human life. When the scales say we do not have enough money to buy wheat, our children die. It was the rich who would not cooperate with Rome. They rebelled and would not cut their vineyards or olive groves to grow the grain. They are the ones who shouted,

"Do not damage the olive oil and the wine!"

It was not because human life was more important; it was because they would not have made as much money raising grain!

Rev. 6:5–6

6:5 When he opened the third seal, I heard the third living creature call out, "Come!" I looked, and there was a black horse! Its rider held a pair of scales in his hand,

6:6 and I heard what seemed to be a voice in the midst of the four living creatures saying, "A quart of wheat for a day's pay, and three quarts of barley for a day's pay, but do not damage the olive oil and the wine!"

---

[19] Roman emperor A.D.81–96 Many believe the Revelation to John was written during this time.

Rev. 6:7–8

6:7 When he opened the fourth seal, I heard the voice of the fourth living creature call out, "Come!"

6:8 I looked and there was a pale green horse! Its rider's name was Death, and Hades followed with him; they were given authority over a fourth of the earth, to kill with sword, famine, and pestilence, and by the wild animals of the earth.

Scene 4

The Lamb opens the fourth seal, and the fourth living creature calls out,

"Come!"

An odor so strong and foul enters the theater, we all think we are going to wretch. Then we see the green horse. I fear I am not conveying to you how putrescent the smell and how vile the color of this horse.

"Its rider's name was Death, and Hades followed with him."

Act two has been building to this horse the whole time. War and violence, malnutrition and starvation are always followed closely by death. Death is not alone on this horse. Behind Death rides Hades, the place of the dead. Hades, a place of no color, no energy, no thought, no creativity, no memories, no pleasure, little interaction. Hades, the place cut off from the living and from God!

The play continues,

"They were given authority over a fourth of the earth, to kill with sword, famine, and pestilence, and by the wild animals of the earth."

We know who death has the authority to kill. It is the Christians who are sentenced to death when they refuse to burn incense to the emperor. The persecution against the Jews in our area has decreased for the time being and they do not have to offer the incense. They pay a tax instead. Other Roman citizens love burning the incense to the emperor, as they think it helps them get ahead in their status as citizens. Other gentiles believe the gods they worship do not care whether they offer the incense, so they do. The Christians are the fourth group and are found to be unpatriotic because they refuse to call Caesar "Lord." The empire never lacks in ways to do violence to the Body of Christ.

The heavenly being told us death has been sent to reap one fourth of the world's people.

We in the audience know that the one-fourth of the people for whom death has come are the Christians. Hades comes with death and "Hades" is the word we Christians use to describe the place of the dead. Death is to take one-fourth of the people by sword, famine, pestilence, and wild animals.

The empire kills the Christians by:

The sword—Everyone in the audience knows someone who has died by the Roman sword.

By famine—Those of us who are Christians can't join the guilds because the guilds eat food offered to idols. As a result we can't get good paying jobs. Without good-paying jobs, we can't afford grain during this time of shortage. We are the poor and the slaves, victims of the famine, made worse by the Romans burning fields around Jerusalem when the city was destroyed.

By pestilence—Along with our hunger, we get contagious diseases from which so many of us have died.

By wild animals—The emperors have Christians wrapped in animal skins, and then exposed to dogs and wild animals to be ripped apart.

How can we not be like the Ephesians and abandon the love we had at first? How can we remember from what we have fallen, and repent, and do the works we did at first? The emperor has declared open season on us, and given death the authority to kill us! But the Lamb is telling us to love our enemies. Love is the power and potency of our faith. This play is showing us how we love and, most importantly, how we love our enemies,[20] is the test of the Christian.

The four primary religious divisions of the Roman Empire as seen from the perspective of a persecuted Christian in 90 A.D.

Christian	Followers of the Roman State religion
Jews	Others

Of these four groups the one fourth to be killed are the Christians

---

[20] Matthew 5:38–48

Rev. 6:7–8

6:7 When he opened the fourth seal, I heard the voice of the fourth living creature call out, "Come!"

6:8 I looked and there was a pale green horse! Its rider's name was Death, and Hades followed with him; they were given authority over a fourth of the earth, to kill with sword, famine, and pestilence, and by the wild animals of the earth.

Rev. 6:9–11

6:9 When he opened the fifth seal, I saw under the altar the souls of those who had been slaughtered for the word of God and for the testimony they had given;

6:10 they cried out with a loud voice, "Sovereign Lord, holy and true, how long will it be before you judge and avenge our blood on the inhabitants of the earth?"

6:11 They were each given a white robe and told to rest a little longer, until the number would be complete both of their fellow servants and of their brothers and sisters, who were soon to be killed as they themselves had been killed.

Scene 5

As we have seen, the four living creatures that surround the throne in the heavenly space each started one of the last four scenes by calling out the word "Come!" I wonder who will call out "Come!" as the curtain again goes up. It is not the voice of a heavenly being we hear as the fifth seal is broken, rather the voices of a great multitude crying out loudly,

"Sovereign Lord, holy and true, how long will it be before you judge and avenge our blood on the inhabitants of the earth?"

The heavenly space fills the stage, and at its center before the throne of the One stands an altar in the shape of a box, with a ram's horn on each corner.

"Under this altar were the souls of those who had been slaughtered for the word of God and for the testimony they had given."

This is the altar the Israelites carried with them in the wilderness as a part of the tabernacle.[21] This is the altar that stood in the temple of Jerusalem.[22] This is the Jewish altar that burned Jewish sacrifices to a Jewish God.[23] Below this Jewish altar rest the souls of two different groups of people. These people are servants who have served the One from the time of Abraham and who are called Jews, and the Brothers and Sisters who are followers of the Lamb, who are called Christians. They are told to rest,

"until the number would be complete both of their fellow servants and of their brothers and sisters, who were soon to be killed as they themselves had been killed."

The altar holds the Jews who have been slaughtered for the word of God in the fall of the Holy City, who have been killed by the empire over the years just for being Jews, the souls of Jews who have been killed for their faith by all the empires of the past.

The altar holds both those Jews and Christians who have

---

[21] Exodus 38:1–2
[22] 2 Chronicles 4:1
[23] 2 Chronicles 7:1–5

been brought before the Roman officials and told to proclaim Caesar as lord, but they would not. The only testimony these Christians would give in the courts of judgement was the testimony to their Lord the Christ. For this treasonous act Christians are executed by the empire. We remember the custom of the Jews to take blood of an animal sacrifice and pour it under the altar.[24] These souls under the heavenly altar,

> "were each given a white robe and told they had to rest a little longer."

We are sad for the way Christians and Jews are being divided in this world. The Romans charge the Jews a tax, which Christians could pay as Jews if the Jews let them. If Christians paid this tax, they would not have to proclaim Caesar as lord. But the rabbis of Jamnia have just issued a change in the synagogue worship. Now Jews are supposed to repeat in their worship "for the Nazarenes may there be no hope."[25] And there are Christians who teach that all Jews are lost, and are no longer loved by God. Then how do we see them here under the same altar, loved with the same love, protected by the same heavenly hosts, waiting for the same justice from the same God? If we are united in heaven, we should not be divided on the earth.

It is a human cry we hear come from the souls under the altar.

> "How long will it be before you judge and avenge our blood?"

We know that this has already been done. The shedding of the blood of Christ's body was an act of judgement and vengeance on the empire, and on all the oppressors of the world.[26] The shedding of the blood of the believers, who are the Body of Christ, is the only way the One will respond to violence.[27] There is redemptive power in the shed blood of martyrs.

---

[24] Leviticus 4:7
[25] Davies, J. G. *The Early Christian Church* (New York: Anchor Books,1967) p. 60.
[26] Romans 12:9–21
[27] Matthew 24:9–14

Rev. 6:9–11

6:9 When he opened the fifth seal, I saw under the altar the souls of those who had been slaughtered for the word of God and for the testimony they had given;

6:10 they cried out with a loud voice, "Sovereign Lord, holy and true, how long will it be before you judge and avenge our blood on the inhabitants of the earth?"

6:11 They were each given a white robe and told to rest a little longer, until the number would be complete both of their fellow servants and of their brothers and sisters, who were soon to be killed as they themselves had been killed.

Rev. 6:12–7:17

6:12 When he opened the sixth seal, I looked, and there came a great earthquake; the sun became black as sackcloth, the full moon became like blood,

6:13 and the stars of the sky fell to the earth as the fig tree drops its winter fruit when shaken by a gale.

6:14 The sky vanished like a scroll rolling itself up, and every mountain and island was removed from its place.

6:15 Then the kings of the earth and the magnates and the generals and the rich and the powerful, and everyone, slave and free, hid in the caves and among the rocks of the mountains,

6:16 calling to the mountains and rocks, "Fall on us and hide us from the face of the one seated on the throne and from the wrath of the Lamb;

6:17 for the great day of their wrath has come, and who is able to stand?"

7:1 After this I saw four angels standing at the four corners of the earth, holding back the four winds of the earth so that no wind could blow on earth or sea or against any tree.

7:2 I saw another angel ascending from the rising of the sun, having the seal of the living God, and he called with a loud voice to the four angels who had been given power to damage earth and sea,

Scene 6

There is a stillness, a quiet anticipation in the audience, as the Lamb breaks the sixth seal.

From the shaking and thunder coming from the stage we hope this sixth scene will be that for which we paid our money. We hope this sixth scene will foretell the day of the Lord, the day when the Holy One will avenge the blood of the martyrs and bring judgment to the earth. We sit on the edge of our seats knowing we will not be disappointed. I promise you my friend, this will be a great scene!

"There came a great earthquake; the sun became black as sackcloth, the full moon became like blood, and the stars of the sky fell to the earth as the fig tree drops its winter fruit when shaken by a gale. The sky vanished like a scroll rolling itself up and every mountain and island was removed from its place. Then the kings of the earth and the magnates and the generals and the rich and the powerful, and everyone, slave and free, hid in the caves and among the rocks of the mountains, calling to the mountains and rocks, 'Fall on us and hide us from the face of the One seated on the throne and from the wrath of the Lamb; for the great day of their wrath has come, and who is able to stand?'"

Then it all stops!
No one is killed!
No one avenged!
It all just stops!
We see,

"An angel, having the seal of the living God and ascending from the rising of the sun calls out with a loud voice to the four angels who had been given the power to damage the earth and sea, saying, 'Do not damage the earth or the sea or the trees, until we have marked the servants of our God with a seal on their foreheads.'"

But we are ready for action. What a disapointment that we will not get to see death come to our enemies! How human we are. We want revenge, but the One is not ready to bring judgment because the One has not finished redeeming. Before the mountains are allowed to fall on human heads or before the four angels who hold back the four winds that will do damage to the earth are allowed to act, the play stops. It stops to remind us that the earth has been bought back, redeemed by the Lamb who is worthy. The earth has been restored to the Kingdom of God. And the call goes out to all,

"enter this Spiritual Kingdom!"

The Holy One intends to take more time to give forgiveness and mercy toward humans who are loved. The audience does not like the fact that the Holy One loves the empire just as unconditionally as the Holy One loves us.

Our judgment and vengeance are put on hold. The four angels with power to harm the earth are told to wait. There are more people to whom the One has to give the seal. God is not finished redeeming us.

"Do not damage the earth or the sea or the trees, until we have marked the servants of our God with a seal on their foreheads."

Some in the audience are surprised to see that the servants to be marked on their foreheads are Jews, Jews from the twelve tribes of Israel. We thought this was a Christian play and here we are told that these Jews are going to heaven. There are both Jews and Christians in the audience, and it is painful to realize that just since the death of Christ so many walls have been built between us: some Christians believing that God no longer loves the Jews, and some Jews believing that for the Christians there is no hope.

We didn't clearly hear the angel announce how many Jews are sealed. Some in the audience think a hundred thousand, some think forty thousand, some say it is a num-

Rev. 7:3–10

7:3 saying, "Do not damage the earth or the sea or the trees, until we have marked the servants of our God with a seal on their foreheads."

7:4 And I heard the number of those who were sealed, one hundred forty-four thousand, sealed out of every tribe of the people of Israel:

7:5 From the tribe of Judah twelve thousand sealed, from the tribe of Reuben twelve thousand, from the tribe of Gad twelve thousand,

7:6 from the tribe of Asher twelve thousand, from the tribe of Naphtali twelve thousand, from the tribe of Manasseh twelve thousand,

7:7 from the tribe of Simeon twelve thousand, from the tribe of Levi twelve thousand, from the tribe of Issachar twelve thousand,

7:8 from the tribe of Zebulun twelve thousand, from the tribe of Joseph twelve thousand, from the tribe of Benjamin twelve thousand sealed.

7:9 After this I looked, and there was a great multitude that no one could count, from every nation, from all tribes and peoples and languages, standing before the throne and before the Lamb, robed in white, with palm branches in their hands.

7:10 They cried out in a loud voice, saying, Salvation belongs to our God who is seated on the throne, and to the Lamb!"

Rev. 7:11–17

7:11 And all the angels stood around the throne and around the elders and the four living creatures, and they fell on their faces before the throne and worshiped God,

7:12 singing, "Amen! Blessing and glory and wisdom and thanksgiving and honor and power and might be to our God forever and ever! Amen."

7:13 Then one of the elders addressed me, saying, "Who are these, robed in white, and where have they come from?"

7:14 I said to him, "Sir, you are the one that knows." Then he said to me, "These are they who have come out of the great ordeal; they have washed their robes and made them white in the blood of the Lamb.

7:15 For this reason they are before the throne of God, and worship him day and night within his temple, and the one who is seated on the throne will shelter them.

7:16 They will hunger no more, and thirst no more; the sun will not strike them, nor any scorching heat;

7:17 for the Lamb at the center of the throne will be their shepherd, and he will guide them to springs of the water of life, and God will wipe away every tear from their eyes."

ber without limit, sealed out of every tribe of the people of Israel.

As arguments break out in the theater over whether or not Jews can be saved, someone yells out,

"I have heard Paul the Apostle say,

'The Jews are beloved for the sake of their ancestors; for the gifts and calling of God are irrevocable.'"[28]

This play will not let us forget the Jews are a part of the Kingdom of God. But they are not alone,

"A great multitude that no one could count, from every nation and from all tribes and peoples and languages, that were standing before the throne and before the Lamb, robed in white, with palm branches in their hands. They cried out in a loud voice, saying, 'Salvation belongs to our God who is seated on the throne, and to the Lamb!'"

There is much joy in heaven knowing that no one will be excluded from the Kingdom of God. A great celebration is taking place. All the angels, the elders, and the four living creatures fall on their faces and sing,

"Amen! Blessing and glory and wisdom and thanksgiving and honor and power and might be to our God forever and ever! Amen'"

One of the elders asks John,

"Who are these, robed in white, and where have they come from?"

John says he does not know, but we know. We know, for the ones robed in white are Christians and Jews who have suffered death at the hands of the empire. They have suffered for their faith; they have suffered as slaves; and they have suffered from the poverty produced by people whose greed knows no limit. Christ bled and died on the cross, and in his bleeding, and in his dying, he bleeds and dies with all who suffer.

---

[28] Romans 11:29

"For this reason they are before the throne of God,
and worship him day and night within his temple,
and the One who is seated on the throne will shelter
them. They will hunger no more, and
thirst no more; the sun will not strike them,
nor any scorching heat;
for the Lamb at the center of the throne will be their
shepherd, and he will guide them to
springs of the water of life,
and God will wipe away every tear from their eyes."

Rev. 8:1

Scene 7

I thank you again, Reader, for coming to this play with
me. As you may have realized this act has come full circle in
the march of time. Act two began with the calling out of the
white horse and its rider, the Holy Spirit of God, who conquered over nothingness to create the universe and all life;
who conquers over violence and sin by giving us Christ who
took the violence of the world upon himself at the cross;
who conquers over death itself by giving us eternal life in
Christ. He came, this rider on the white horse, carrying the
bow of the clouds, a promise not to destroy, but to redeem.

Then came war, with the rider of the red horse. It was
Cain that gave this rider permission to take peace from the
earth, Cain, the brother of Abel. Since that ancient tale was
told, Cain still lives in the hearts of all who wish the death of
their brothers and sisters. This part of us called Cain lives in
our hearts, and rises up when we are angry, and shouts to
the rider of the red horse,

"Kill! Kill! We want them dead!"

The third horse carried that monstrous child abuser,
famine. Famine followed close behind war and has followed
war since the beginning of time. It has been official policy of
governments since the beginning to count the soldiers' bodies, but they do not bother to count the children, old people,
women, and men who were victims of the battle through
famine.

Next in time came death. Death, the rider of the green
horse, comes to claim the weak and hungry and give them
to Hades, a place where the dead reside. In this play we are
told it is a pale green horse that death rides. Pale green, the
mirror image of how we will look when death has come for
us.

In scene five, we saw the souls of the dead who wait for
the Day Of The Lord. These souls call out,

"How long, O Lord, how long?"

They are asking the questions everyone in the audience
is asking:

"How long will you allow violence and famine and death to rule the earth? How long before you avenge us on our enemies? How long before you stop this madness of war and death?"

In the sixth scene the time had come for time to end. The time had come for the Day Of The Lord. The time had come for revenge and payback. What a great day it was going to be! In the sixth scene, the sun goes black, the sky is rolled up, and the mountains and rocks are to fall on the heads of kings. The adrenaline flows in our veins as we watch this great scene take place. Now is the day we get even for ourselves and for those who have already suffered and died. Then it all stops!   The sixth scene is interrupted. The great scene for which we have waited and wanted is put on hold. The angels are told that nothing is to be hurt, because the One has not finished redeeming us. Then all the hosts of heaven begin to sing the new song taught them by the cow who has many eyes and six wings.

Someday the Garden created by the rider of the white horse, before peace was taken from the earth, will be restored.

One of the elders says to John,

"and the One who is seated on the throne will shelter them. They will hunger no more, and thirst no more; the sun will not strike them, nor any scorching heat; for the Lamb at the center of the throne will be their shepherd, and he will guide them to springs of the water of life, and God will wipe away every tear from their eyes."

That's real nice, but our adrenaline is still flowing and we want the Day Of The Lord! We want those mountains and rocks to fall on the heads of the kings! In this seventh scene we want our revenge! The curtain opens. It is the seventh and last scene in this second act. The human (Cain) part of us is ready for blood, and as the seventh seal is broken,

"there is silence in heaven for about half an hour."

Time to think, time to pray, time to realize,
God has not finished redeeming us.

Here Ends the Second Act

Rev. 8:1

8:1 When the Lamb opened the seventh seal, there was silence in heaven for about half an hour.

Rev. 10:8–11

10:8 Then the voice that I had heard from heaven spoke to me again, saying, "Go, take the scroll that is open in the hand of the angel who is standing on the sea and on the land."

10:9 So I went to the angel and told him to give me the little scroll; and he said to me, "Take it, and eat; it will be bitter to your stomach, but sweet as honey in your mouth."

10:10 So I took the little scroll from the hand of the angel and ate it; it was sweet as honey in my mouth, but when I had eaten it, my stomach was made bitter.

10:11 Then they said to me, "You must prophesy again about many peoples and nations and languages and kings."

Sweet In The Mouth Bitter In The Stomach

Hurt
He wants them hurt.
His playmates called him names.
Hate now plans the hurt.
How pleasing is the thought!

If he could, he would.
In time he will.
It will happen.
Instead of he, she went with him.
Indeed he will get even.
Inspired by the thought.

Just try to keep him home.
June first he is to go.
Jumping from airplanes behind the lines.
Jabbing and stabbing.
Justified by faith and family.
Justice must be done.
Joy in the thought.

Kill them!
Knock them in the head!
Knife them in the stomach!
Knowing you are right
Knee-deep in blood.
Keeping alive the thought.

Life is lost.
Love is lost.
Lost is pleasure, inspiration, joy.
Loathsomeness remains.
Let go the thought.

Act III

Rev. 8:2–11:18

The Setting

Seven angels stand before the One seated on the throne in heaven in this setting for the third act. Each of the seven angels is given a trumpet. Someone yells, "These are the seven archangels," and different people start calling out their names, "Raguel," "Michael and Sariel," "Gabriel," "Remiel, Uriel and Raphael."

You see, my friend, the Jews in the audience believe these are their seven archangels and call out their names. This naming of the angels is another way for Christians in the audience to know this play is also for the Jews. We are being shown in this play that when something happens in the heavenly court it happens for both Jews and Christians.

An eighth angel is given a golden censer and offers to the One the prayers of all the saints, mixed with incense. The saints pray a lot, for the angel is given

"a great quantity of incense to offer with the prayers of all the saints on the golden altar that is before the throne."

We can see that the heavenly space did not change with the birth of Christ. The angels, the living creatures, the golden censer and golden altar, the hosts of heaven who worship the One are part of the same heavenly vision seen by the Jews.

And now,

"the smoke of the incense, with the prayers of the saints, rose before God from the hand of the angel."

This eighth angel took

"fire from the altar and threw it on the earth; and there were peals of thunder, rumblings, flashes of lightning, and an earthquake."

Rev. 8:2–6

8:2 And I saw the seven angels who stand before God, and seven trumpets were given to them.

8:3 Another angel with a golden censer came and stood at the altar; he was given a great quantity of incense to offer with the prayers of all the saints on the golden altar that is before the throne.

8:4 And the smoke of the incense, with the prayers of the saints, rose before God from the hand of the angel.

8:5 Then the angel took the censer and filled it with fire from the altar and threw it on the earth; and there were peals of thunder, rumblings, flashes of lightning, and an earthquake.

8:6 Now the seven angels who had the seven trumpets made ready to blow them.

Rev. 8:2–6

8:2 And I saw the seven angels who stand before God, and seven trumpets were given to them.

8:3 Another angel with a golden censer came and stood at the altar; he was given a great quantity of incense to offer with the prayers of all the saints on the golden altar that is before the throne.

8:4 And the smoke of the incense, with the prayers of the saints, rose before God from the hand of the angel.

8:5 Then the angel took the censer and filled it with fire from the altar and threw it on the earth; and there were peals of thunder, rumblings, flashes of lightning, and an earthquake.

8:6 Now the seven angels who had the seven trumpets made ready to blow them.

The One wants attention! Something very important is about to happen and the One wants the audience to be alert, for the seven angels are preparing to blow their trumpets. The ram's horns are used by the Jews to signal all important events and seasons. The ram's horn, the trumpet, is also used to signal the excommunication of someone from the community.

It was a Caesar who gave the order to burn Jerusalem. It was a Caesar who declared open season on the Christians. It was a Caesar who was proclaimed Son of God, and issued coins that said so. It is Caesar's empire that is so large and so powerful that temples are built to the city of Rome itself, and people worship the god Roma. If some people are to be convinced once and for all that Caesar is not the Son of God, that the city of Rome is not a god, and the empire is not the earthly reflection of the Heavenly Kingdom, it is going to take a lot of trumpet-blowing, many peals of thunder, rumblings, flashes of lightning, and a *big* earthquake!

The archangels of heaven are about to blow the rams' horns to signal the excommunication of the emperor and the empire. Not only are they going to be excommunicated from the true community of faith, but those of us watching this play hope that the emperor and the empire are excommunicated from life itself. We are ecstatic that the empire is about to get what it deserves. Now the third of the land on the earth that is the empire is going to be judged.

The earth divided into thirds.

Scene I

As the curtain opens on the first scene of act three, the first trumpet of excommunication is heard.

Revenge, what sweet revenge, comes in this third act. My friend, can you feel the sweetness of the revenge? The angels are going to use the Jewish trumpet of excommunication to excommunicate the Roman empire. Hail is falling on the empire. Hail that is like the rocks that fell upon the Christians, and on the besieged Jews of Jerusalem. Fire falls upon the one third of the earth which is the Roman empire. All the empire's trees are burned up and all the empire's grass is burned up, and all the empire is burned up. The same fire that burned the life out of the Christians and provided light for Nero's gardens at night. The same fire that burned the city of Jerusalem and its temple, resulting in the death of at least six hundred thousand Jews. This fire is mixed with blood. Rome and the empire can not be separated from blood. This is not new blood, or blood created by the One to throw down from heaven. This is our blood, the blood of the Christians and Jews that the empire has shed. Blood collected from the innocents and held until this day when the lives of the believers will be avenged. The audience is on their feet, shouting, whistling, cheering, applauding as the empire burns![1]

Rev. 8:7

8:7 The first angel blew his trumpet, and there came hail and fire, mixed with blood, and they were hurled to the earth; and a third of the earth was burned up, and a third of the trees were burned up, and all green grass was burned up.

---

[1] See note number one.

Rev. 8: 8–9

Rev. 8:8 The second angel blew his trumpet, and something like a great mountain, burning with fire, was thrown into the sea.

Rev. 8:9 A third of the sea became blood, a third of the living creatures in the sea died, and a third of the ships were destroyed.

Scene 2

The second ram's horn sounds.

Yes! The empire is being excommunicated! At last my friend, the ships of the empire are destroyed. There are no more fish for the empire. The arteries of commerce that carry life to the god Roma have burst. The shipping lanes clot. They coagulate from the blood of those carried to their death like the Christians, Jews and slaves who have been carried off to Rome to be brutalized and killed by the empire. Their deaths were not only physical; it is also the death of their spirits as they live the life of prisoners and slaves. Now their blood, and the blood of all who have died in the production of goods for Rome, sent on ships, has been thrown down like a great mountain upon the sea, and choked the sea until it could not live, until the sea swallowed all those ships.

"Freedom now! Freedom from the ships!"[2]

---

[2] See note number two for an explanation of shipping in the Roman Empire.

Scene 3

"The third angel blew his trumpet, and a great star fell from heaven, blazing like a torch, and it fell on a third of the rivers and on the springs of water. The name of the star is Wormwood. A third of the waters became wormwood, and many died from the water, because it was made bitter."

The truth is being exposed to us in this scene, my friend. The trumpet of excommunication, the ram's horn of faithfulness is sounding the call, and now the empire is to be judged. Of what is the empire accused? Unfaithfulness; fornication with idols. King Herod was unfaithful right here in Judea when he had statues set up to the Roman god-emperor Augustus. The empire requires each of us to offer a pinch of incense to the emperor to prove loyalty, and to declare "Caesar is Lord." To do so is to be unfaithful to our God of Creation, the Giver of Life. To call the emperor "Lord" is to deny our true Lord, Jesus of Nazareth. To force those who would work in the guilds to eat meat offered to idols at guild meals is to force the workers to commit fornication with false gods.[3] The empire burned the temple and the city of Jerusalem, so now they believe their own gods to be stronger and our God, Yahweh, destroyed. They created the god Roma out of the empire itself.

And the emperors! Some are called gods while they are yet alive. Emperor Nero erected a colossus of the sun with his own features in front of his Golden House. Nero is that star that falls from heaven blazing like a torch, whose name is Wormwood, and who turns the water bitter. The empire prostitutes itself to false gods. The empire is guilty of being unfaithful to the One who is over all, Lord of Lords and King of Kings. The empire must now drink the bitter waters to test their guilt or innocence.

"And many died from the water, because it was made bitter."

Are you feeling, my friend the reader, that this is what you want to see? Proof that our enemy deserves to die. A test to show their guilt. In this test of bitter water let the empire sit bare-breasted before the Lord, and be condemned as the curtain falls.[4]

---

[3] Ezekiel 16:15 and 20:4–5

[4] See note number three for the test of bitter waters.

8:10 The third angel blew his trumpet, and a great star fell from heaven, blazing like a torch, and it fell on a third of the rivers and on the springs of water.

8:11 The name of the star is Wormwood. A third of the waters became wormwood, and many died from the water, because it was made bitter.

Rev. 8: 12–13

8:12 The fourth angel blew his trumpet, and a third of the sun was struck, and a third of the moon, and a third of the stars, so that a third of their light was darkened; a third of the day was kept from shining, and likewise the night.

8:13 Then I looked, and I heard an eagle crying with a loud voice as it flew in midheaven, "Woe, woe, woe to the inhabitants of the earth, at the blasts of the other trumpets that the three angels are about to blow!"

Scene 4

Now the fourth trumpet of excommunication is heard, and the fourth scene of act three begins. As the curtain opens a darkness is felt by the audience, slowly pushing out the light.

I hope you can feel the darkness as the audience feels it. There is no sun over the empire. The sun has been struck from its place just like the emperor Nero has been struck down. He made himself into the sun and thought himself a god, and was struck from the throne at the age of thirty-one, forced to try and take his own life before it was taken from him.[5]

The darkness is more than the death of the sun god Nero. The darkness is remembering the empire has killed six hundred thousand Jews in the destruction of Jerusalem. The darkness is remembering that the Holy City, Jerusalem, has been knocked down and burned. The darkness is remembering that the temple, built by King Herod, has been desecrated and burned. The darkness is remembering that tens of thousands of Jews, young and old, have been chosen for death because they cannot work. The darkness is remembering that as we sit in this theater watching this play, tens of thousand of Jews, as well as countless others, are working as slaves in mines and fields all around the empire, victims of the Roman army. Six thousand of those Jewish slaves worked for Nero digging the Corinth canal. The darkness is remembering that thousands of Jews have been sent around the empire to be killed in hippodromes by gladiators and wild beasts. These Jews were our brothers, our fathers, mothers, sisters. They were family, if not in blood, then in faith.

This darkness is the darkness that comes with remembering our leaders. Our beloved Lord, hung on a cross by the Romans.

"James, the son of Zebedee, put to death with the sword by Herod Agrippa. Simon Peter, crucified with his head downward, under emperor Nero. Paul beheaded at Rome under Nero. Aristarchus, a traveling companion of Paul, slain at Rome, under Nero. Epa-

---

[5] See note number 4: Nero as Sun God

phras slain by Nero. Prisca, Aquila, Andronicus, and Junia martyred in Rome by Nero. Onesiphorus, a friend of Paul, and Porphyrius, his companion, tied to wild horses and dragged, or torn, to death, at Hellespontus, through the edict of Nero. Others slain by Nero: Prochorus, Nicanor, Parmenas, Olympus, Carpus, Trophimus, Maternus and Egystus, Marianus, Hermagoras, Onesimus, Dionysius, Areopagitae, and others, also died at the time for the divine truth."[6]

There is no moon or stars for Nero to drive his chariot among, for they too have been struck dark.[7] How dark the night! Who can look at the beauty of the heavens, who can lift their head weighed down with mourning, remembering Nero, Domitian and the empire. There is no light over the empire. There never is light over the head of a tyrant. There never will be light where there is no freedom and justice.

John continues the play,

"Then I looked, and I heard an eagle crying with a loud voice as it flew in midheaven. 'Woe, woe, woe to the inhabitants of the earth, at the blasts of the other trumpets that the three angels are about to blow!'"

Can we believe this eagle? We have seen it flying at the head of each legion of Roman soldiers, on their shields and standards, on their buttons and belts. It is the symbol of the empire. It has loaned its power and majesty to the rot that is Rome. Or did the Romans steal from this majestic bird, as they have stolen from unnumbered tribes and peoples of the earth? Now the One has reclaimed the eagle, called it back to the heavens. The One has called back the eagle from the Romans, restored its strength, renewed its power, set it free to fly, and to cry, "Woe, woe, woe, you inhabitants of the earth!" To warn us, the empire has not finished with the pain it will cause. To warn the empire, they must listen for the trumpets. Listen for the angels to blow the trumpets.

Rev. 8: 12–13

8:12 The fourth angel blew his trumpet, and a third of the sun was struck, and a third of the moon, and a third of the stars, so that a third of their light was darkened; a third of the day was kept from shining, and likewise the night.

8:13 Then I looked, and I heard an eagle crying with a loud voice as it flew in midheaven, "Woe, woe, woe to the inhabitants of the earth, at the blasts of the other trumpets that the three angels are about to blow!"

---

[6] van Braght, Thieleman, The Bloody Theater or Martyrs Mirror of the Defenseless Christians (Scottdale, Pennsylvania: J. Herald Press, 1950) p. 79.

[7] See note number 5: Nero Among the Stars

Rev. 9:1–12

9:1 And the fifth angel blew his trumpet, and I saw a star that had fallen from heaven to earth, and he was given the key to the shaft of the bottomless pit;

9:2 he opened the shaft of the bottomless pit, and from the shaft rose smoke like the smoke of a great furnace, and the sun and the air were darkened with the smoke from the shaft.

9:3 Then from the smoke came locusts on the earth, and they were given authority like the authority of scorpions of the earth.

9:4 They were told not to damage the grass of the earth or any green growth or any tree, but only those people who do not have the seal of God on their foreheads.

9:5 They were allowed to torture them for five months, but not to kill them, and their torture was like the torture of a scorpion when it stings someone.

9:6 And in those days people will seek death but will not find it; they will long to die, but death will flee from them.

9:7 In appearance the locusts were like horses equipped for battle. On their heads were what looked like crowns of gold; their faces were like human faces,

9:8 their hair like women's hair, and their teeth like lions' teeth;

9:9 they had scales like iron breastplates, and the noise of their wings was like the noise of many chariots with horses rushing into battle.

Scene 5

The audience hears again those words from scene four,

"There are no moon nor stars for Nero to drive his chariots among, for they too have been struck dark. How dark the night! Who can look at the beauty of the heavens, who can lift their head, weighed down with mourning, remembering Nero, Domitian and the empire. There is no light over the empire. There never is light over the head of a tyrant. There never will be light where there is no freedom, where there is no justice."

With darkness as the backdrop, the fifth angel blows the trumpet of excommunication. The audience is taken back in time, back to the Creation, to the beginning of things, to the time of the red horse and its rider. The rider of the red horse is given permission to take peace from the earth.

First we gave permission to the rider of the red horse to take peace from the earth, and now we give permission to the star fallen from heaven to take peace from the earth by using the key to the bottomless pit. This star fallen from heaven like a blazing torch, whose name is Wormwood, turns the water bitter.

Hissing, the audience vents their anger at the star they recognize as the emperor Nero.

Those of us in the audience remember that Nero proclaimed himself a god and had his image in the form of a star god placed in the entry to his golden palace. This star, this god, this Nero is not in the heavens; he fell from heaven and unlocked the shaft of the bottomless pit. He let the rider of the red horse loose upon the earth.

Our theater fills with smoke and stench. We cup hands over faces to escape the foulness coming from the bottomless pit.

"The sun and the air were darkened with the smoke from the shaft."

We hear the sounds, sounds of humans being torn by wild beasts. We see the glow and smell smoke, the smoke from human flesh burning. Here before us, on this stage, is revealed the true nature of the god Roma. This false god is a pit, a hole, a vacuum that pulls into itself our wealth, our energy, our leaders, our freedom, and, all too often, our lives.

Out of the pit come creatures. Legions and legions and legions of creatures. Are these Roman Legions human? Through the smoke we see their heads have a different shape, their bodies shine like human skin cannot, and they surely have no hearts. They swarm over the earth like locusts,[8]

"and they were given authority like the authority of scorpions of the earth."

They do not eat the grass or trees, but worse—in villages, towns, cities, on the seas, and along the frontiers of the empire these locusts stand ready to force their will by pain and torture. They look for the Christians, the Christians who do not have the seal of God on their foreheads as do the Jews. They seek out the Christians who do not have the seal of the empire on their foreheads as do those citizens who have offered their incense to the emperor.

We are the ones, the Christians, that these legion-locusts spend their entire lives pursuing. They do not have the authority to kill us. Instead they take us for trial; then, after the trial they are told they can kill us as traitors.

And who leads these legions of locusts? The angel of the bottomless pit, Abaddon in Hebrew or Apollyon in Greek. In either language, the name means destroyer. The destroyer is a human, a ruler, an emperor!

No one can have power over another unless that person first destroys the dreams and freedom of the one made subject.

Heard in the darkness of the theater:

"These times are dark, these times are filled with pain! The locusts of darkness and the legions of pain come for me! O, that I were dead!"

The first woe is passed. There are still two woes to come. Count them, count the woes, and you will understand that the One has not finished redeeming us.

---

[8] See note number six. An army described as locusts in The Old Testament.

Rev. 9:10–12

9:10 They have tails like scorpions, with stingers, and in their tails is their power to harm people for five months.

9:11 They have as king over them the angel of the bottomless pit; his name in Hebrew is Abaddon, and in Greek he is called Apollyon.

9:12 The first woe has passed. There are still two woes to come.

Rev. 9:13–11:14

9:13 Then the sixth angel blew his trumpet, and I heard a voice from the four horns of the golden altar before God,

9:14 saying to the sixth angel who had the trumpet, "Release the four angels who are bound at the great river Euphrates."

9:15 So the four angels were released, who had been held ready for the hour, the day, the month, and the year, to kill a third of humankind.

9:16 The number of the troops of cavalry was two hundred million; I heard their number.

9:17 And this was how I saw the horses in my vision: the riders wore breastplates the color of fire and of sapphire and of sulfur; the heads of the horses were like lions' heads, and fire and smoke and sulfur came out of their mouths.

9:18 By these three plagues a third of humankind was killed, by the fire and smoke and sulfur coming out of their mouths.

Scene 6

As the curtain opens on scene six, we all lean forward not wanting to miss a word in anticipation and hope of sweet vengeance. We can feel the tension.

For the sixth time the empire is excommunicated by the sounding of the trumpet. Excommunicated for its unfaithfulness to God, to the One above all others, to the Creator. Excommunicated for pretending its leaders are gods who come from the stars. Then we hear it, a voice! A voice so loud, so powerful, so enveloping it is heard in the far corners of the heavens. The voice comes from the golden altar with the four horns. It is the voice of all who have been sacrificed on the altar of tyranny. Those whose souls have waited under the altar of the One, and who have cried out unceasingly,

"How long, O Lord, how long!"

Now is their day, for now they shout to the angel with the trumpet,

"Release the four angels who are bound at the great river Euphrates."

Those are the four angels who were held back until the servants of God could be marked on their foreheads.

"The four angels who had been held ready for the hour, the day, the month and the year, to kill a third of humankind."

Now they can be released on the third of the earth controlled by the empire. On all those in the empire who do not believe: those who betray believers in order to steal their possessions; those who arrest believers, those who prosecute them, those who judge them, those who jail them, those who murder them; those who make the laws that allow this to take place; those who sit back and do nothing to stop the injustice. The guilty ones, the sinful ones, the lost ones, they are the citizens of the empire, who will be destroyed.

We are not disappointed. Two hundred million of God's heavenly cavalry descend on the empire. What an army they are! The Greek fire and sulfur bombs used by the empire are now used against the empire by the heavenly army! The riders of the heavenly horses blaze with fire and sapphire, and the horses, like dragons, breathe fire and smoke and sulfur.

"By these three plagues a third of humankind was killed, by the fire and smoke and sulfur coming out of their mouths."

The audience is on their feet. Their cheering and yelling, clapping and whistling, shake the theater. There are tears of joy in every eye. What a sweet, sweet day. Strangers hugging and trading kisses. What a joy the coming of an army of two hundred million! What a joy the death of the citizens of the empire! The rest of the earth, we are told, will continue to go their old ways.

A light! What is this light? Why is it blocking our view of the carnage? We came to see the play. We came to see the death. We want our sweet vengeance. The light is blinding bright; we can no longer see what is happening on the stage. Once again this great scene is taken from us, as it was when the four angels were told to wait after the sixth seal was broken. The audience is hissing again. We want the carnage, we want the sweet death!

Now we see the form of a great angel. Its face is like the sun, its legs pillars of fire, and its brightness has blocked our view of the stage. This angel has a rainbow over his head. The rainbow is the sign of peace, the sign the One gave the Jews to remind us that the One is a God of creation, and not destruction. He stands with one foot on the land and one on the water, for the One has created and loves them both. He shouts so loud the seven thunders sound. He has to shout, for in our heads we still hear the glory of the war between the empire and two hundred million heavenly troops.

The noise of the battle is so loud we cannot make out what the angel says. John is told not to write it down, but with the shout of the angel all slowly becomes quiet.

The audience sits back down and stops their hissing. The sound of the battle could no longer be heard in their heads. A silence fell over the theater. The angel then

Rev. 9:19–10:6

9:19 For the power of the horses is in their mouths and in their tails; their tails are like serpents, having heads; and with them they inflict harm.

9:20 The rest of humankind, who were not killed by these plagues, did not repent of the works of their hands or give up worshiping demons and idols of gold and silver and bronze and stone and wood, which cannot see or hear or walk.

9:21 And they did not repent of their murders or their sorceries or their fornication or their thefts.

10:1 And I saw another mighty angel coming down from heaven, wrapped in a cloud, with a rainbow over his head; his face was like the sun, and his legs like pillars of fire.

10:2 He held a little scroll open in his hand. Setting his right foot on the sea and his left foot on the land,

10:3 he gave a great shout, like a lion roaring. And when he shouted, the seven thunders sounded.

10:4 And when the seven thunders had sounded, I was about to write, but I heard a voice from heaven saying, "Seal up what the seven thunders have said, and do not write it down."

10:5 Then the angel whom I saw standing on the sea and the land raised his right hand to heaven

10:6 and swore by him who lives forever and ever, who created heaven and what is in it, the earth and what is in it, and the sea and what is in it: "There will be no more delay,

Rev. 10:7–11

10:7 but in the days when the seventh angel is to blow his trumpet, the mystery of God will be fulfilled, as he announced to his servants the prophets."

10:8 Then the voice that I had heard from heaven spoke to me again, saying, "Go, take the scroll that is open in the hand of the angel who is standing on the sea and on the land."

10:9 So I went to the angel and told him to give me the little scroll; and he said to me, "Take it, and eat; it will be bitter to your stomach, but sweet as honey in your mouth."

10:10 So I took the little scroll from the hand of the angel and ate it; it was sweet as honey in my mouth, but when I had eaten it, my stomach was made bitter.

10:11 Then they said to me, "You must prophesy again about many peoples and nations and languages and kings."

"raised his right hand to heaven and swore by the One who lives forever and ever, who created heaven and what is in it, the earth and what is in it, and the sea and what is in it: 'There will be no more delay, but in the days when the seventh angel is to blow his trumpet, the mystery of God will be fulfilled, as he announced to his servants the prophets.'"

The audience is happy to hear there will be no more delay, for we feel we have been put off too long. Twice now the great scene of destruction has been put on hold or interrupted. In our minds it is time to complete the scene of sweet destruction.

John is told by a voice from heaven to go and take the scroll that is in the hand of the angel. As he did so he is told to eat it, and is warned it will be

"sweet in the mouth, but bitter in the stomach."

He found it to be true when he ate the scroll; it was sweet as honey in his mouth, and bitter in his stomach.

He is told he

"must prophesy *again* about many peoples and nations and languages and kings."

There is no movement, no sound from the audience for what seems a long time. Then they begin to talk among themselves.

"What has happened? Why did the angel not allow the empire to be destroyed? Why did John have to prophesy again? What was wrong with what he said the first time?"

Someone in the audience yells,

"John has made a mistake. He has shown us how sweet is the death of the empire. He has forgotten how bitter will be the pain in its dying; that is the message of the scroll. How sweet the thought of the empire burning and the sea turned to blood, how bitter to smell the smoke and see the death!"

John is told to preach again.

As much as we in the audience want it to happen, we know the Roman empire is not to die in this Act. The One loves the empire as much as the One loves us. All that happened in the last five scenes happened out of our lust for revenge, and those scenes were sweet to imagine but would be bitter in reality. Those scenes cannot really happen, for the One is not finished redeeming the empire.

We in the audience have been wrong. It is not sweet revenge we are promised by our Lord, but the tough directive to love the empire.[9] The empire is preserved because God has not finished redeeming it.

The audience starts talking among themselves again.

"We came to see the empire destroyed, and now we are told we must learn to love it!"

As the audience continues to grumble their attention is drawn back to the stage where John has just been given a staff. He is to measure the temple of God in Jerusalem.

Who in the audience can forget the vicious way the temple and city have so recently been destroyed by the Romans? Hundreds of thousands of Jews have been slaughtered or carried off as slaves.

Here on the stage a replica of the temple and city have been built. They have the women's court, the men's court, the priests' court, the porch, the Holy Place and the Holy of Holies of the temple on the stage. The outer courts are left off to be trampled upon by the nations.

The empire may have destroyed Jerusalem and Herod's temple, but now those of us in the audience can see the Holy of Holies belongs to the One, and can still be measured. God's presence with the human family on the earth can still be measured.

A nation of souls starts across the stage. Souls of men and women and children who have been slaughtered because they are Jews. These souls are seen in the form of two great witnesses who have the authority to prophesy for as long as evil lasts. No matter what the empire does, the spirit of the One remains alive and present with the human family.

[9]Matthew 5:38–48

Rev. 11:1–6

11:1 Then I was given a measuring rod like a staff, and I was told, "Come and measure the temple of God and the altar and those who worship there,

11:2 but do not measure the court outside the temple; leave that out, for it is given over to the nations, and they will trample over the holy city for forty-two months.

11:3 And I will grant my two witnesses authority to prophesy for one thousand two hundred sixty days, wearing sackcloth."

11:4 These are the two olive trees and the two lampstands that stand before the Lord of the earth.

11:5 And if anyone wants to harm them, fire pours from their mouth and consumes their foes; anyone who wants to harm them must be killed in this manner.

11:6 They have authority to shut the sky, so that no rain may fall during the days of their prophesying, and they have authority over the waters to turn them into blood, and to strike the earth with every kind of plague, as often as they desire.

Rev. 11:7–14

11:7 When they have finished their testimony, the beast that comes up from the bottomless pit will make war on them and conquer them and kill them,

11:8 and their dead bodies will lie in the street of the great city that is prophetically called Sodom and Egypt, where also their Lord was crucified.

11:9 For three and a half days members of the peoples and tribes and languages and nations will gaze at their dead bodies and refuse to let them be placed in a tomb;

11:10 and the inhabitants of the earth will gloat over them and celebrate and exchange presents, because these two prophets had been a torment to the inhabitants of the earth.

11:11 But after the three and a half days, the breath of life from God entered them, and they stood on their feet, and those who saw them were terrified.

11:12 Then they heard a loud voice from heaven saying to them, "Come up here!" And they went up to heaven in a cloud while their enemies watched them.

11:13 At that moment there was a great earthquake, and a tenth of the city fell; seven thousand people were killed in the earthquake, and the rest were terrified and gave glory to the God of heaven.

11:14 The second woe has passed. The third woe is coming very soon.

Moses and Elijah, the two olive trees, the two great witnesses, who stand forever before the Lord,

"And if anyone wants to harm them, fire pours from their mouth and consumes their foes[10] . . . could shut the sky, so that no rain may fall during the days of their prophesying,[11] and they have authority over the waters to turn them into blood and to strike the earth with every kind of plague,[12] as often as they desire."

Those of us in the audience are reminded how, in the year 67, the beast Nero sent the general Vespasian to destroy Jerusalem. Three and one half years later the city fell, and the carnage that took place during and after the fall of Jerusalem was one of the empire's greatest evils. Its intensity revealed the true nature of the god Roma. They let the dead bodies of the Jews lie in the streets of that once great city.

"And the inhabitants of the earth gloated over them and celebrated and exchanged presents, because these two prophets had been a torment to the inhabitants of the earth."

But it is not to last. God did not leave them hopeless. The breath of life from the One enters them. The two prophets and all the souls within them, all the Jews, hear the loud voice,

"Come up here!"

And they go up to heaven in a cloud while their enemies watch.

"At that moment there was a great earthquake, and a tenth of the city fell; seven thousand people were killed in the earthquake, and the rest were terrified and gave glory to the God of heaven."

The earthquake is the earthquake of the Roman Army that has shaken this part of the world since before any of us can remember. After this Roman earthquake John was told seven thousand people were killed. What it means is that

---

[10] 2 Kings 1: 9–10
[11] I Kings 17:1
[12] Exodus 7:17, 19

Jerusalem was annihilated. Seven is the complete number, and signifies to those of us in the audience that there were none left. They killed most of them in the three and a half year siege, many after the fall of Jeruslam, and drove off the rest who were terrified but still gave glory to the God of heaven.

We thought at the beginning of this scene the heavenly calvary of two hundred million would wipe out the empire. What joy we felt at the thought! Then the angel came and told us that was a mistake. He told us that the One was not finished redeeming the empire and that we must learn to love it. Now are we also to love the Jews? In this play we are constantly reminded to include the Jews, that the One is with them, and calls them into the heavenly presence. The One calls them into heaven not because they have become Christian, but because they are Jews.

The second woe is passed; the third woe is coming. Watch for it and you will understand that the One has not finished redeeming us.

Rev. 11:15–18

11:15 Then the seventh angel blew his trumpet, and there were loud voices in heaven, saying, The kingdom of the world has become the kingdom of our Lord and of his Messiah, and he will reign forever and ever."

11:16 Then the twenty-four elders who sit on their thrones before God fell on their faces and worshiped God,

11:17 singing, We give you thanks, Lord God Almighty, who are and who were, for you have taken your great power and begun to reign.

11:18 The nations raged, but your wrath has come, and the time for judging the dead, for rewarding your servants, the prophets and saints and all who fear your name, both small and great, and for destroying those who destroy the earth."

Scene 7

The angel said in scene six of act three,

"There will be no more delay, but in the days when the seventh angel is to blow his trumpet, the mystery of God will be fulfilled, as he announced to his servants the prophets."

The audience is not sure we want to see the curtain rise on this Seventh Scene, for we were promised in scene six that with the blowing of the seventh trumpet the mystery of God would be fulfilled. And what is this mystery? Will the empire finally be destroyed? Will people be set free and live with peace and justice? Again we sit on the edge of our seats as the curtain goes up.

The seventh angel blows his trumpet

Voices chant, voices so rapturous, so powerful, so loud that they are louder than the trumpet, louder than any sound the audience can make, so loud you may be able to hear them where you are, my friend. Loud voices chant at the raising of the curtain:

> "The kingdom of the world has become the kingdom
> of our Lord and of his Messiah, and He will reign
> forever and ever"

On the stage the twelve apostles and twelve elders of Israel, who sit on their thrones before God, fall on their faces and worship God, singing,

> "We give you thanks, Lord God Almighty, who are and who were, for you have taken your great power and begun to reign."

So this is the mystery of God that would be fulfilled! Caesar, the strongest tyrant on the face of the earth, is excommunicated. Cast out! Cast down from the heavens he thought were his. And now Caesar must call the One, the One who is not man, not woman, the One who is other, the One who is light, the One who is color, Caesar must call the One, Lord.[13]

---

[13] Philippians 2:9–11

The audience is once again on their feet. They are cheering and dancing, for now they belong to a new Kingdom. Not the kingdom of the Caesars, not the kingdom of Nero or Domitian, not the kingdom of any Caesar yet to come. Not the kingdom of any human person who has lived, or lives, or will live. They belong to the Kingdom of God, the Kingdom of the One who rules in human hearts. This is freedom. This is justice.

The nations will rage,[14] but it is the One who will judge. It is the One who will reward the servant prophets and all the saints (Jews and Christians) who have waited beneath the heavenly altar. Reward them with a life of peace and justice that does not end. It is the One who will cause to fall all the false stars who think they are "lords."

Here Ends the Third Act

Rev. 11:15–18

11:15 Then the seventh angel blew his trumpet, and there were loud voices in heaven, saying, The kingdom of the world has become the kingdom of our Lord and of his Messiah, and he will reign forever and ever."

11:16 Then the twenty-four elders who sit on their thrones before God fell on their faces and worshiped God,

11:17 singing, We give you thanks, Lord God Almighty, who are and who were, for you have taken your great power and begun to reign.

11:18 The nations raged, but your wrath has come, and the time for judging the dead, for rewarding your servants, the prophets and saints and all who fear your name, both small and great, and for destroying those who destroy the earth."

---

[14] Psalms. 46:6

It is a Rule.
These Beasts and Dragons
Can Only Have the Power
We Give Them.

Red dragon,
Master of
Life and death.
Sweeps away
The stars
Waits with open mouth
To eat
Children
At their birth

A beast
Below,
In the bottomless pit,
Where boils
Hells' billowing blasts

Another,
A second, servant beast
With power to kill
Humans,
Who do not worship
That beast from the pit

A tale of supernatural horrors?

Or just a tale
Of life
In the empire,
In any empire,
In every empire

How easy if it were only a
Dragon,
But it is the empire's tail
That sweeps away the stars.
The empire
Waits to eat the child

The emperor,
All emperors,
Our emperor,
Lives in the pit
Filled
With the smoke
Of burning martyrs

The second beast
An unholy priest
With power to kill
Those
Who will not worship
Caesar

What of the killer Satan
And slanderer Devil?
Who are they?
Forgive me, Lord,
And grant it so
Their name
Be not mine.

Act IV

Rev. 11:19–15:4

Rev. 11:19

11:19   Then God's temple in heaven was opened, and the ark of his covenant was seen within his temple; and there were flashes of lightning, rumblings, peals of thunder, an earthquake, and heavy hail.

The Setting

Jerusalem has fallen and Rome still rules the land of Israel. Rome rules the Jews who had not been killed or hauled off to slavery around the empire or fed to wild beasts in the hippodromes of the empire's great cities.

Reader, don't you think it was good to learn in the last act that the Jews would be called up to share the heavenly space? But what about the Jews on earth? How can we sing the Lord's song in this strange and painful place?[1] We need God here with us. We need something to remind us of God's presence. We need the prophet Moses to pray for us as he did so long ago at Sinai:

It is written of Moses in Deut. 9: 25– 29

"Throughout the forty days and forty nights that I lay prostrate before the Lord when the Lord intended to destroy you, I prayed to the Lord and said, 'Lord God, do not destroy the people who are your very own possession, whom you redeemed in your greatness, whom you brought out of Egypt with a mighty hand. Remember your servants, Abraham, Isaac, and Jacob; pay no attention to the stubbornness of this people, their wickedness and their sin, otherwise the land from which you have brought us might say, 'Because the Lord was not able to bring them into the land that he promised them, and because he hated them, he has brought them out to let them die in the wilderness. For they are the people of your very own possession, whom you brought out by your great power and by your outstretched arm.'"

---

[1] Psalm 137

78

And in Deut. 10: 1– 2

"At that time the Lord said to me, 'Carve out two tablets of stone like the former ones, and come up to me on the mountain, and make an ark of wood. I will write on the tablets the words that were on the former tablets, which you smashed, and you shall put them in the ark.'"

We need the prophet Moses to go back up the mountain, among the flashes of lightning, rumblings, peals of thunder, earthquakes, and heavy hail, and again talk with the Lord. We need the prophet Moses to be given the law on stone tablets, and to put them again in the ark of the covenant. The ark was proof that the One who is our God loves us, guides us and protects us, and is here and present with us in the face of all the adversity yet to come.

There, before us on the stage, now appears the backdrop of the scenes to come in the fourth act:

"Then God's temple in heaven was opened, and the ark of his covenant was seen within his temple."

Here is proof, the proof of faith, that God is with us always. The ark of the covenant is revealed to us in the heavenly temple. It does not matter how Rome, or any empire, treats the earthly ark of the covenant, for there is an ark eternal in the heavens. Now the One is with us. Now we know we can go on to meet any dragon or beast, for God is always present with us. This ark is our proof.

11:19   Then God's temple in heaven was opened, and the ark of his covenant was seen within his temple; and there were flashes of lightning, rumblings, peals of thunder, an earthquake, and heavy hail.

Rev. 12:1–17

12:1 A great portent appeared in heaven: a woman clothed with the sun, with the moon under her feet, and on her head a crown of twelve stars.

12:2 She was pregnant and was crying out in birthpangs, in the agony of giving birth.

12:3 Then another portent appeared in heaven: a great red dragon, with seven heads and ten horns, and seven diadems on his heads.

Scene I

The only way I can describe to you what happens next is to say the audience is shocked into silence as the curtain opens for the first scene of the fourth act. There appears on the stage in front of the ark,

"a woman clothed with the sun, with the moon under her feet, and on her head a crown of twelve stars."

It was the emperor Nero who gave the impression through his Colossus that he was the sun. It was the emperor Nero who drove his chariot among the moon and stars on the ceiling of the great theater. It was the emperor Nero who minted coins with his crown of sunbeams and stars. It was the emperor Nero who started the persecution of the Christians, and who ordered the destruction of Jerusalem.

In your imagination, can you see on this stage a woman clothed like the emperor himself? The audience came to their feet shouting, hoping and believing that the woman did not only look like the emperor, but had taken the emperor's power. What a revolutionary thought! A woman should replace the emperor.

How we cheered when we realized this woman is Israel. Around her head is the crown of the twelve tribes. This woman is the faith, the history, the tradition, the pain, and the joy of Israel. It is in the faith and life of this woman Israel that true power and freedom are to be found, not in the emperor.

This woman Israel,

"was crying out in her birthpangs, in the agony of giving birth."

Again the audience comes to their feet as a huge, bloody dragon with open mouths waddles slowly toward the pregnant Israel. There is no doubt in the minds of the audience what this dragon is. They see this bloody dragon with its seven heads and ten horns many times every day. It stands in the markets of our towns and villages holding spears it uses to oppress.

This dragon sits at tables in the markets and along the roads to collect taxes which are sent to the bottomless pit. This bloody dragon takes the crops of the poor farmers and sails the ships which take the food to Rome and away from the hungry. It carries the mail, with orders from the emperor to further tax and oppress, or kill. This dragon builds and runs the jails, tortures the Christians, cooks for the army, sits as judges, rules as prefects and kings subject to the emperor. This bloody dragon is the empire itself. The dragon is anyone who works for the empire and helps it carry out its bloody plans. The oppression by this bloody dragon is so severe, and the air so filled with smoke of burning bodies, that the stars are no longer visible. All beauty of nature, all joy of life, and for many all reason to live, is stolen by the bloody dragon.

This despicable creature

"stood before the woman who was about to bear a child, so that he might devour her child as soon as it was born."

The audience is hissing and shaking their fists as they see in their minds that bloody dragon-empire who arrested, tried, and crucified their Lord. They shout their anger at the dragon that destroyed the Sacred City and chased the few Jews who remained into a wilderness exile where they seek the nourishment of God. This bloody dragon stands ready to devour the child of Israel, as every bloody dragon before and since stands ready to devour the children of the poor and oppressed.

"And she gave birth to a son, a male child, who is to rule all the nations with a rod of iron. But her child was snatched away and taken to God and to his throne; and the woman fled into the wilderness where she has a place prepared by God, so that there she can be nourished for one thousand two hundred sixty days."

How many of Israel's children have been snatched away? There is no end to this list. What of Jerusalem? How many times has the dragon destroyed Jerusalem?

The bloody dragon is not to win. It thinks itself a god. It calls itself a god and requires worship from people of the empire. Then,

Rev. 12:4–7

12:4 His tail swept down a third of the stars of heaven and threw them to the earth. Then the dragon stood before the woman who was about to bear a child, so that he might devour her child as soon as it was born.

12:5 And she gave birth to a son, a male child, who is to rule all the nations with a rod of iron. But her child was snatched away and taken to God and to his throne;

12:6 and the woman fled into the wilderness, where she has a place prepared by God, so that there she can be nourished for one thousand two hundred sixty days.

12:7 And war broke out in heaven; Michael and his angels fought against the dragon. The dragon and his angels fought back,

Rev. 12:8–12

12:8 but they were defeated, and there was no longer any place for them in heaven.

12:9 The great dragon was thrown down, that ancient serpent, who is called the Devil and Satan, the deceiver of the whole world— he was thrown down to the earth, and his angels were thrown down with him.

12:10 Then I heard a loud voice in heaven, proclaiming, Now have come the salvation and the power and the kingdom of our God and the authority of his Messiah, for the accuser of our comrades has been thrown down, who accuses them day and night before our God.

12:11 But they have conquered him by the blood of the Lamb and by the word of their testimony, for they did not cling to life even in the face of death.

12:12 Rejoice then, you heavens and those who dwell in them! But woe to the earth and the sea, for the devil has come down to you with great wrath, because he knows that his time is short!"

"a war broke out in heaven; Michael and his angels fought against the dragon. The dragon and his angels fought back, but they were defeated, and there was no longer any place for them in heaven. The great dragon was thrown down, that ancient serpent, who is called the Devil and Satan, the deceiver of the whole world—he was thrown down to the earth, and his angels were thrown down with him."

Joy, undiluted joy fills the hearts and tears of the audience. What a celebration takes place in this theater! God has told us what we have always known: "THERE IS NO HOLY EMPIRE!" The bloody dragon who is the empire is cast out of heaven. There is not now, there was never before, there never will be, a holy empire. Empires are by their nature bloody, and are daily cast out of heaven.

We hear the loud voice:

"Now have come the salvation and the power and the kingdom of our God and the authority of his Messiah."

The audience is dancing, for now is the Kingdom come, now is the Messiah Lord of all, making us truly free of the bloody dragon.

"For the accuser of our comrades has been thrown down, who accuses them day and night before our God. But they have conquered him by the blood of the Lamb and by the word of their testimony, for they did not cling to life even in the face of death."

Now those souls under the altar can rejoice, for as they, like their Lord, have died, in their death they have conquered and have bought life and freedom from the dragon. The play continues,

"Rejoice then, you heavens and those who dwell in them. But woe to the earth and the sea, for the devil has come down to you with great wrath, because he knows that his time is short."

But there is more to this first scene. Dragons are always sore losers. The bloody dragon is very angry and again goes after the woman Israel. The audience is on their feet cheering for the woman, as the One gives her "the two wings of the great eagle, so that she could fly from the serpent into the wilderness, to her place where she is nourished for a time, and times, and half a time."

Not only does the woman take the appearance away from the emperor, but the One gives her the eagle,[2] the bird of the empire with which to escape. The very bird said to have carried emperor Augustus into heaven. No matter how in control and powerful the bloody dragon seems to be, the One is in charge, and ultimately brings victory.

As the woman flees the dragon, the dragon opens its mouths and a great river pours out. The audience can see that this is not a river of water, but of men, men that the audience have seen so often before. As this army of men flows over the countryside like a great river, the earth itself comes to the aid of the woman. The earth swallows up the army. And so it has been and so it is. No matter how great or powerful the dragon, no matter how large the army, the earth will eventually swallow it up. Nero and Domitian killed the Jews who kept the commandments, and Christians who held the testimony of Jesus. The emperors force the bloody dragon to make war on the rest of Israel's children.

Rev. 12:13–17

12:13   So when the dragon saw that he had been thrown down to the earth, he pursued the woman who had given birth to the male child.

12:14   But the woman was given the two wings of the great eagle, so that she could fly from the serpent into the wilderness, to her place where she is nourished for a time, and times, and half a time.

12:15   Then from his mouth the serpent poured water like a river after the woman, to sweep her away with the flood.

12:16   But the earth came to the help of the woman; it opened its mouth and swallowed the river that the dragon had poured from his mouth.

12:17   Then the dragon was angry with the woman, and went off to make war on the rest of her children, those who keep the commandments of God and hold the testimony of Jesus.

---

[2] Isaiah 40:31

Rev. 12:18–13:10

12:18 Then the dragon took his stand on the sand of the seashore.

13:1 And I saw a beast rising out of the sea, having ten horns and seven heads; and on its horns were ten diadems, and on its heads were blasphemous names.

13:2 And the beast that I saw was like a leopard, its feet were like a bear's, and its mouth was like a lion's mouth. And the dragon gave it his power and his throne and great authority.

13:3 One of its heads seemed to have received a death-blow, but its mortal wound had been healed. In amazement the whole earth followed the beast.

13:4 They worshiped the dragon, for he had given his authority to the beast, and they worshiped the beast, saying, "Who is like the beast, and who can fight against it?"

13:5 The beast was given a mouth uttering haughty and blasphemous words, and it was allowed to exercise authority for forty-two months.

13:6 It opened its mouth to utter blasphemies against God, blaspheming his name and his dwelling, that is, those who dwell in heaven.

13:7 Also it was allowed to make war on the saints and to conquer them. It was given authority over every tribe and people and language and nation,

Scene 2

It is lower this time, but with more power, more intensity. The hissing from the audience is one unending, slow serpentine swell. Scene Two begins at the seashore with the bloody dragon standing on the sand. It is the dragon the audience denounces with their hissing.

Vivid in our minds is the picture of the angel of God who gave John the small scroll to eat. He stood with one foot on the sea and one on the land because the One had created them both and had power over both. This dragon thinks it has power over all, but stands only on the sand.

Use your imagination, my friend, and you can watch a beast rising out of the sea. It is more sinister than the beast of Daniel,[3] for it has all the qualities of Daniel's four beasts combined in one.

"It had ten horns, and was like a leopard, its feet were like a bear's, and its mouth was like a lion's mouth."

On its ten horns are ten diadems and on its heads are blasphemous names, the names we are required to call the emperor: divine, son of god, saviour, lord, god, or saviour of the world. We are to declare, "Caesar is lord," or face death. The audience grows quiet out of fear of the beast.

The empire in the form of the bloody dragon now gives to the beast,

"his power and his throne and great authority."

Powerful tyrants get their power from those they govern. That power is often taken back by the dragon and given to another, as the Roman Senate revolted against Nero's rule and took his power. As so many of the conquered lands tried to revolt against the empire. As the Jews revolted against an emperor who thought himself a god.

The audience knows when we see the wounded head of the beast that this beast is the emperor. We recognize the wounded head as the emperor Nero, for many believe he did not die but will come from the east with a great army

---

[3] Daniel 7:1–8

and take back the empire. How we hate Nero! It is hard to believe these two creatures, the god Roma and the emperor, are worshiped by most of the people in the empire.

> "Who is like the beast," they would ask, "and who can fight against it?"

The emperor beast blasphemes God and all that God means to the people in the audience. He calls himself God, and believes heaven belongs to himself. In the back of our minds we know as we watch this beast that even emperor beasts have limits. We know that the One will arrange in "a time, times, and half a time" to have the emperor beast swallowed up.

On the stage this beast plays out the war on the Christians, killing them, torturing them, hunting them down like wild animals. It plays out this war on all people. This oppression is felt by every tribe and tongue in the empire. There is no one exempt from the beast's system of cruelty. And through time, before this system is done, all the earth, all whose names are not faithful and true, will be forced to worship the beast in one way or another, in one country or another, in one age or another.

The audience is unusally quiet in the face of the murderous beast. How can we respond to such all-powerful tyranny?

A voice from the stage answers this unspoken question.

> "Let anyone who has an ear listen:
> If you are to be taken captive,
> into captivity you go;
> If you kill with the sword,
> with the sword you must be killed.
> Here is a call for the endurance and faith of the saints."

This is not a voice the audience wants to hear. Telling us we may have to endure captivity, torture, or death while feeling love for those who are our captors, our torturers, or our executioners. The voice is telling us if we are to be taken captive, we must go and take our blows

Rev. 13:8–10

13:8 and all the inhabitants of the earth will worship it, everyone whose name has not been written from the foundation of the world in the book of life of the Lamb that was slaughtered.

13:9 Let anyone who has an ear listen:

13:10 If you are to be taken captive, into captivity you go; if you kill with the sword, with the sword you must be killed. Here is a call for the endurance and faith of the saints.

"while not losing the love we had at first."[4]

If we decide to take up arms, we take on the face of the beast and will die by the rules of the earthly empire. We will not be a part of the Kingdom of God.

---

[4] Revelation 2:4

Scene 3

Again the stage is dark, with only a glimmer of light coming from the east as though it were dawn.

We see movement on the stage in this third scene. We see, rising up from the earth, yet another beast. As it rises onto the stage we see its two horns, giving the impression of a lamb. We are not fooled; we know the Lamb of God is Jesus our Lord. Then it speaks with a voice of the dragon. As the beast becomes fully visible, it is not hard to discern what it is.

This second beast presides over the yearly celebrations and feeds us meat from those tables, meat we cannot eat, meat that cries out its pain from being sacrificed to gods who are not gods. What celebrations they have! It is difficult not to attend and take part. These beasts work wonders. They can make the image of the emperor speak and they, like Elijah, can make fire come down from heaven. These beasts from the earth are the great high priests in the temple of the state. Many of us in the audience are holding our heads in pain, for we know that we can't go to these great celebrations. We cannot call the emperor "Lord." We know what will happen to those of our faith who have been identified as enemies of the state because they will not take part, will not offer incense, will not proclaim Caesar "Lord." We know the great high priests will condemn us to death.

We know these priests because the emperor has sent them as vassal kings or proconsuls, to all the countries of the Roman empire, small and large, to rule those countries in the emperor's name.

They serve as both priests and kings, both priests and proconsuls. They are both priests and procurators, priests and prefects, priests and magistrates. They have the voice of the dragon empire and the power of the emperor. This beast from the earth forces us to do homage to the emperors.

This beast forces believers to call the emperor lord, when we have only one Lord, the Christ.[5] And if we do not wor-

13:11 Then I saw another beast that rose out of the earth; it had two horns like a lamb and it spoke like a dragon.

13:12 It exercises all the authority of the first beast on its behalf, and it makes the earth and its inhabitants worship the first beast, whose mortal wound had been healed.

13:13 It performs great signs, even making fire come down from heaven to earth in the sight of all;

13:14 and by the signs that it is allowed to perform on behalf of the beast, it deceives the inhabitants of earth, telling them to make an image for the beast that had been wounded by the sword and yet lived;

13:15 and it was allowed to give breath to the image of the beast so that the image of the beast could even speak and cause those who would not worship the image of the beast to be killed.

---

[5] See note number four: a description of how a proconsul priest forces the Christians to their deaths.

Rev. 13:16–18

13:16 Also it causes all, both small and great, both rich and poor, both free and slave, to be marked on the right hand or the forehead,

13:17 so that no one can buy or sell who does not have the mark, that is, the name of the beast or the number of its name.

13:18 This calls for wisdom: let anyone with understanding calculate the number of the beast, for it is the number of a person. Its number is six hundred sixty-six.

ship, we cannot trade, for we do not get the seal of the emperor that shows we have made our vows. We cannot buy or sell, we cannot join the trades. We are condemned by this beast to a life of poverty.

What magic these priests have, how they love mystery, how they love to deceive, to make us wonder. They tell us the number of the beast. From its number we must learn its name. But we know the name. We know the name of this beast is Neron Caesar.[6] We do not know the names of the many beasts yet to come, but we do know they will share the number that is not perfect, 666.

---

[6] The numerical equivalent of Nero in Latin is N-50, E-6, R-500, O-60, N-50, Neron Caesar, the total comes to 666. In Hebrew the letters of Nero Caesar also add up to 666.

Scene 4

It may not be possible to relate to you everything that is going to happen, because those of us in the theater are hiding our eyes from the play going on before us. The dragon and the two beasts are more than we want to watch. The audience looks at each other, looks up or down, anywhere except the stage.

Music begins to carry us away from this theater, music that calms us and melts our fear. Singing begins this fourth scene, singing like we have never heard before in any language. Its beauty is the sound of a child's cry at birth, its rhythm is the rhythm of an infant laughing. The song's language is the language of a child so young it speaks the words of God.

As we look up to the stage, we see our children. We see our children who have been slaughtered at the fall of the Holy City. Children who have been murdered by the violent mobs who surround our homes and communities. We see our children who have died in the murderous life of slavery, children who have died of starvation and disease. We see our children who have had their life crushed out of them by the weight of the empire, by the weight of past empires, by the weight of empires yet to come. We see our children who have been taken from us because of the madness of men called Caesar.

These children are surrounding the Lamb on Mount Zion, following the Lamb and singing like the male singers of Mount Zion before the temple was burned.[7] Our children have a place as first fruits in the presence of God. What joy and tears sweep the audience. Our boys and girls, our babies, our infants, our children occupy the very center of the play. Our play is half over, half yet to be seen, and here in the middle of it all are the children. We must not forget the children! Of all the heavenly hosts; the Jews, the people of every language, and tribe, and tongue, the creatures of all creation are present before God, and we must not forget the children. They sing a song before the throne and before the four living creatures and before the elders, and no one can learn their song for it is the very language of God.

---

[7] I Chronicles 6:31–48

Rev. 14:1–5

14:1 Then I looked, and there was the Lamb, standing on Mount Zion! And with him were one hundred forty-four thousand who had his name and his Father's name written on their foreheads.

14:2 And I heard a voice from heaven like the sound of many waters and like the sound of loud thunder; the voice I heard was like the sound of harpists playing on their harps,

14:3 and they sing a new song before the throne and before the four living creatures and before the elders. No one could learn that song except the one hundred forty-four thousand who have been redeemed from the earth.

14:4 It is these who have not defiled themselves with women, for they are virgins; these follow the Lamb wherever he goes. They have been redeemed from humankind as first fruits for God and the Lamb,

14:5 and in their mouth no lie was found; they are blameless.

Rev. 14: 6–13

14:6 Then I saw another angel flying in midheaven, with an eternal gospel to proclaim to those who live on the earth—to every nation and tribe and language and people.

14:7 He said in a loud voice, "Fear God and give him glory, for the hour of his judgment has come; and worship him who made heaven and earth, the sea and the springs of water."

14:8 Then another angel, a second, followed, saying, "Fallen, fallen is Babylon the great! She has made all nations drink of the wine of the wrath of her fornication."

14:9 Then another angel, a third, followed them, crying with a loud voice, "Those who worship the beast and its image, and receive a mark on their foreheads or on their hands,

14:10 they will also drink the wine of God's wrath, poured unmixed into the cup of his anger, and they will be tormented with fire and sulfur in the presence of the holy angels and in the presence of the Lamb.

14:11 And the smoke of their torment goes up forever and ever. There is no rest day or night for those who worship the beast and its image and for anyone who receives the mark of its name."

14:12 Here is a call for the endurance of the saints, those who keep the commandments of God and hold fast to the faith of Jesus.

Scene 5

It is not a smell. It is too strong, too hot for a smell. It is a burning of the nose, the face, the eyes. Lime, it is lime mixed with the plants and water for tanning that causes this discomfort in the audience in scene five. It is the burning of the pigs' hides to remove the hair. It is the burning of tons of wood to make charcoal.

There were small fires to cook and keep warm, hot fires to fire pottery, and hotter fires to make iron. On the stage they show the fires, the fires of the empire. They are everywhere people live. They are everywhere people resist the power of the beast. On the frontier in France, Germany, England, and Bithynia, humans are burned alive. Homes are set on fire with families inside, while the accused is forced to watch. Their stores of grain are destroyed by fire. Their cities and towns are burned to bring submission to the god Caesar.

And there were the big fires: the Holy City, Jerusalem, an inferno. The temple burned with victims trapped inside. Huge sulfur balls were thrown through the air at the city, bursting into flame upon impact. Flaming sulfur arrows struck human beings, killing twice. All the fields around the city for as far as a person could see were set on fire by the Romans to destroy Jerusalem's food.

Rome itself was on fire. Block after block, mile after mile of the city burned to the ground. The fire would be blamed on the Christians, a fire that would lead to the death of Christians by burning. Believers were fastened to stakes with pitch poured on them, set afire so the emperor could see in the dark. This is the smoke of the empire. It is the smoke that never stops, that has risen day and night for three hundred years in the empire. It will continue to rise as long as empires last and believe they have the right to burn human flesh.

Can you see the guilty on the stage, all those who worship the beast, who offer their pinch of incense, who receive the mark of the beast? They are a part of the evil dragon. They are forced to live in the squalor. They want to survive, they want to make a living. They have no power, they say, to stop or change the dragon and its beasts. They are condemned to breathe for all time this hot, putrid air of the empire. This condemnation is the very wine of God's wrath. It is the blood of the believers and innocents that is the wine of God's wrath poured unmixed into the cup of his anger. In this play God does not need to do something to humans to vent anger. The One only needs to let the consequences of human actions take their toll. God's wrath is felt on the earth in the actions of humans. This living hell, this torment, is witnessed by the holy angels and by the Lamb.

The loud voice of an angel is heard in the theater. The voice is calling all present, all who believe, to endure, to hang on, to not give up, not give in. Stay separate from the business of the empire which is the business of killing, enslaving and burning human beings. A call to those of us who are Jews, keep the commandments no matter how terrible the smoke of the empire on this earth. A call to those of us who are Christians, hold fast to the faith of Jesus even when arrested and led out to the flames of the empire. This angel calls out to all who live on the earth, to every nation and tribe and language and people, even those who live in the empire with the mark of the beast upon them.

> "Fear God and give him glory, for the hour of his judgment has come; and worship him who made heaven and earth, the sea and the springs of water."

God does not desire that humans should live in the hell of an empire, so God continuously sends the angels to remind us of our redemption.

> "Then we hear the second angel calling out 'Fallen, fallen is Babylon the great! She has made all nations drink of the wine of the wrath of her fornication.'"

We are all in this together. All people in this audience, from every tribe, and nation, and language have been led away from the One by the empire who made us drink the blood of the martyrs. All who profit in any way from the empire are guilty of drinking the blood of the martyrs. The empire expects us to accept their death without protest or action. Christians who have been made to offer incense, to deny their faith when challenged, and who have refused to

Rev. 14:13

14:13 And I heard a voice from heaven saying, "Write this: Blessed are the dead who from now on die in the Lord." "Yes," says the Spirit, "they will rest from their labors, for their deeds follow them."

hide the believers from the empire, have been forced by the empire to drink a double portion of the wine of the wrath of her fornication.

A third angel calls, "There is no rest day or night for those who worship the beast and its image, and for anyone who receives the mark of its name."

A heavenly voice gives a blessing at the close of this scene.

"Blessed are the dead who from now on die in the Lord."
   "Yes," says the Spirit, "they will rest from their labors, for their deeds do follow them."

Scene 6

My friend, we have arrived at yet another sixth scene. The audience is ready. Our patience is short. In the last two acts we have prepared to see the end of the empire in the sixth scene, and that end has been stolen from us by God's redeeming acts toward the empire. Now is the time. We have been promised in act three that there would "be no more delay." We want to see the blood of the empire overflow the stage. We want to hear the empire's cries of mortal pain.

On the stage there appears one like the Son of Man, wearing a golden crown on his head, seated on a white cloud, and carrying a sickle.

At this sight the audience jumps to their feet with loud cheers. We know that this one like the Son of Man is our Christ, our redeemer, and that he will use that sickle against the empire.

The audience becomes quiet as an angel comes out of the heavenly temple.

"Use your sickle and reap, for the hour to reap has come, because the harvest of the earth is fully ripe." So the one who sat on the cloud swung his sickle over the earth, and the earth was reaped.

The audience is cheering so loud and so long that the play has to pause until order can be restored. We are so anxious to see the empire punished! We want our vengeance.

There is quiet as

"another angel came out of the temple in heaven, and he too had a sharp sickle."

Someone yells,

"What can this mean, for the earth has already been reaped?"

Rev. 14:14–20

14:14 Then I looked, and there was a white cloud, and seated on the cloud was one like the Son of Man, with a golden crown on his head, and a sharp sickle in his hand!

14:15 Another angel came out of the temple, calling with a loud voice to the one who sat on the cloud, "Use your sickle and reap, for the hour to reap has come, because the harvest of the earth is fully ripe."

14:16 So the one who sat on the cloud swung his sickle over the earth, and the earth was reaped.

14:17 Then another angel came out of the temple in heaven, and he too had a sharp sickle.

14:18 Then another angel came out from the altar, the angel who has authority over fire, and he called with a loud voice to him who had the sharp sickle, "Use your sharp sickle and gather the clusters of the vine of the earth, for its grapes are ripe."

14:19 So the angel swung his sickle over the earth and gathered the vintage of the earth, and he threw it into the great wine press of the wrath of God.

14:20 And the wine press was trodden outside the city, and blood flowed from the wine press, as high as a horse's bridle, for a distance of about two hundred miles.

Rev.14:14–20

14:14 Then I looked, and there was a white cloud, and seated on the cloud was one like the Son of Man, with a golden crown on his head, and a sharp sickle in his hand!

14:15 Another angel came out of the temple, calling with a loud voice to the one who sat on the cloud, "Use your sickle and reap, for the hour to reap has come, because the harvest of the earth is fully ripe."

14:16 So the one who sat on the cloud swung his sickle over the earth, and the earth was reaped.

14:17 Then another angel came out of the temple in heaven, and he too had a sharp sickle.

14:18 Then another angel came out from the altar, the angel who has authority over fire, and he called with a loud voice to him who had the sharp sickle, "Use your sharp sickle and gather the clusters of the vine of the earth, for its grapes are ripe."

14:19 So the angel swung his sickle over the earth and gathered the vintage of the earth, and he threw it into the great wine press of the wrath of God.

14:20 And the wine press was trodden outside the city, and blood flowed from the wine press, as high as a horse's bridle, for a distance of about two hundred miles.

Another angel, who has authority over fire, comes out of the temple and

"called with a loud voice to the angel who had the sharp sickle, 'Use your sharp sickle and gather the clusters of the vine of the earth, for its grapes are ripe.'"

The angel then gathers the vintage of the earth.

Who is this vintage of the earth, and why are there two reapings of the earth? It is difficult for the audience to accept what they are seeing. They want the empire to be killed. They want the empire to be cut in half by the reaper's sickle. But those who have been harvested are not the murderers of the empire. The audience can see now who it is the Son of Man and the angel have reaped. The Son of Man has harvested the grain of the earth, Christians who are followers of the Way[8] from all the gentile world! The Angel has harvested the clusters of the Jews from the vine of Israel, spread abroad on the face of the earth.

How can this be? We feel betrayed, tricked into thinking there is justice in this play. This is the third act in which the sixth scene has let us down.

The audience moans with horror at what happens next. Those believers who have been harvested from the earth are thrown to the lions, crucified and burned alive before our eyes. It is their blood that begins to overflow the stage. The blood of the believers does not stop flowing until it has covered the entire countryside for as far as the eye can see, and deep as a horse's head.

It is this evil, this evil winepress that presses the life out of the faithful and produces the wine which will one day choke the empire. This is the blood of God's wrath the empire will drink to become drunk, and lay poisoned in their guilt.

The audience is angry for it is now clear that God's wrath is not going to end the empire with the sword. But we, the believers, must redeem the empire by accepting the sword upon ourselves, as Christ accepted death on the cross.

---

[8] Acts 9:2

In the silence of the audience's anger, someone near the back of the theater calls out,

"We have just seen the Eucharist. At the supper of our Lord, Jesus took bread made of grain, broke it and said this is my body broken for you, and likewise after the meal he took a cup filled with the fruit of the vine, blessed it and passed it to his disciples saying, all of you drink of this for this is my blood shed for you and for many for the forgiveness of sins. The gentile grain and the Jewish fruit of the vine we have just seen reaped and thrown into the winepress of the empire become the spiritual nourishment that gives life to us all. We must be willing to give ourselves for the kingdom of God."

Rev. 15:1–4

15:1 Then I saw another portent in heaven, great and amazing: seven angels with seven plagues, which are the last, for with them the wrath of God is ended.

15:2 And I saw what appeared to be a sea of glass mixed with fire, and those who had conquered the beast and its image and the number of its name, standing beside the sea of glass with harps of God in their hands.

Scene 7

A somber and quiet audience waits for the curtain to open for the seventh scene.

We are not quite sure what has just happened, not sure if we want to give up our lives in order to redeem an empire we hate. We are not sure we can endure the persecutions to come with the love we had at first.[9] We are not sure we understand how our blood can become the *wrath* of God.

Yet we know our God is a God of justice. We know when injustice is done, time has a way of catching up with the perpetrator of that injustice. We want to believe that patient endurance will see the Kingdom of God come upon the earth.

The curtain goes up and there is

"another portent in heaven, great and amazing."

Seven angels with seven plagues! What a confusion there is in the audience, for these plagues are to be the last, and with them the wrath of God would end. We wonder if that means the persecutions of the believers will stop? If that is what is meant we are happy. Or does it mean that now the empire is going to get what it has coming? Either way we will be happy, my friend, will you?

With the magic of drama there

"appeared to be a sea of glass mixed with fire, and those who had conquered the beast and its image and the number of its name, standing beside the sea of glass with harps of God in their hands."

People in the audience begin to call out, for they see their loved ones who have been thrown into the winepress of the wrath of God and are now standing in the heavenly space. These who have come through the baptism of the glassy sea into the very presence of God. We can see that the flames of their torment followed them even into that sacred space, but the flames cannot hurt them. The two groups of

---

[9] Revelation 2:4

believers, the Jewish grapes harvested by an angel of the heavenly temple and the gentile grain harvested by one like the Son of Man, are now singing the song of Moses, the servant of God, and the song of the Lamb.

They sing,

"Great and amazing are your deeds, Lord God the Almighty! Just and true are your ways, King of the nations!"

They are right about the amazing part. How more amazing can it get, that the way to punish the empire is to take the punishment of the empire upon ourselves, just as Christ did on the cross?

They sing that

"All nations will come and worship before you, for your judgments have been revealed."

The audience is not sure about this one. What will nations think if they know our God takes the punishment for sin upon Christ and the believers? Yet God alone is Holy, and in that holiness we must place our faith.

Here Ends the Fourth Act

Rev. 15:3–4

15:3 And they sing the song of Moses, the servant of God, and the song of the Lamb: Great and amazing are your deeds, Lord God the Almighty! Just and true are your ways, King of the nations!

15:4 Lord, who will not fear and glorify your name? For you alone are holy. All nations will come and worship before you, for your judgments have been revealed."

Rev. 16:12–16

16:12   The sixth angel poured his bowl on the great river Euphrates, and its water was dried up in order to prepare the way for the kings from the east.

16:13   And I saw three foul spirits like frogs coming from the mouth of the dragon, from the mouth of the beast, and from the mouth of the false prophet.

16:14   These are demonic spirits, performing signs, who go abroad to the kings of the whole world, to assemble them for battle on the great day of God the Almighty.

16:15   ("See, I am coming like a thief! Blessed is the one who stays awake and is clothed, not going about naked and exposed to shame.")

16:16   And they assembled them at the place that in Hebrew is called Harmagedon.

Madness

A young man's called to hunt, to fight, to kill.
Men, women, children, nature are his foes.
The day has come to call the caller ill.

Romantic with his sword, or gun, or kilt.
As reason from his brain so freely flows,
A young man's called to hunt, to fight, to kill.

Battles and bombs and bayonets leave chills,
When follows severed arms, and heads, and toes.
The day has come to call the caller ill.

Shells loud and hot and blinding bright and shrill.
War smells of feet, of shit, of puke, so goes
A young man called to hunt, to fight, to kill.

The spoils of war are in the raven's bill
Or trapped within young bodies laid in rows.
The day has come to call the caller ill.

The farmers look across the field to till.
They wonder if the corn from new bones grows.
A young man's called to hunt, to fight, to kill
The day has come to call the caller ill.

Act V

Rev. 15:5–16:21

Rev. 15:5–16:1

15:5 After this I looked, and the temple of the tent of witness in heaven was opened,

15:6 and out of the temple came the seven angels with the seven plagues, robed in pure bright linen, with golden sashes across their chests.

15:7 Then one of the four living creatures gave the seven angels seven golden bowls full of the wrath of God, who lives forever and ever;

15:8 and the temple was filled with smoke from the glory of God and from his power, and no one could enter the temple until the seven plagues of the seven angels were ended.

16:1 Then I heard a loud voice from the temple telling the seven angels, "Go and pour out on the earth the seven bowls of the wrath of God."

The Setting

Many have now left the theater. They are angry at this play. Angry that the blood of the wrath of God is the spilling of the blood of the believers. They paid good money to see their enemies suffer tortuous pain and death at the command of the One. Now they have been told that it is *their* suffering that will be redemptive for the empire. They do not want the empire redeemed; they want the empire dead. Will you stick it out with me, my friend, or are you also upset?

The stage hands are setting the stage for the fifth act. They are pulling out to the center of the stage the temple of the Tent of Witness that is in heaven. It is filled with smoke so we know the One must be present. When the One is there it fills with the smoke from the glory of God and from God's power, just as the Tent of Witness used to do in the wilderness with Moses.

From the Tent of Witness come seven angels. Their clothing is so bright, so white, it is difficult to look at them. They have gold sashes across their chests. One of the four living creatures gives the seven angels seven golden bowls full of the wrath of God. We all strain to see if the bowls hold the blood of the martyrs, the blood that is the wrath of the One who lives forever and ever. This must be the wrath of God that John had mentioned in the previous act. This is the last, for with this blood the wrath of God will be ended, done, finished. There will be no more.[1]

> "No one can enter the temple until the seven plagues of the seven angels are ended."

---

[1] See preface on the wrath of God.

It's too bad people have left the theater, for now surely we are going to see what God really wants us to see. Now we will see what is going to happen to the empire.

A loud voice from the temple tells the seven angels,

"Go and pour out on the earth the seven bowls of the wrath of God."

Rev. 16:2

16:2 So the first angel went and poured his bowl on the earth, and a foul and painful sore came on those who had the mark of the beast and who worshiped its image.

Scene I

They elevated the stage for this act, and now before us is the scene of the heavenly temple and the seven angels with their seven golden bowls standing in front. The first angel comes to the edge of the stage and pours the bowl down upon the earth. We can see that every one who has the mark of the beast on the earth is affected by this bowl of God's wrath. They break out in sores, big, ugly, foul sores.

At first the audience just sits silently. This is pretty anticlimactic when expecting the wrath of God to be poured out. These are just sores. Then someone starts to chant.

"Let my people go, let my people go, let my people go! Let my people go!"

These are the sores Moses and Aaron caused to come upon the Egyptians in the sight of Pharaoh.[2] These were the sores that helped free the people of Israel from slavery in the past. So now will these sores help free the believers from the slavery of Rome? Will these sores lead to freedom from slavery imposed by empires yet to come? You may be able to hear the audience, for we are all chanting, "Let us go, let us go, let all the people go!"

---

[2] Exodus 9: 10 So they took soot from the kiln, and stood before Pharaoh, and Moses threw it in the air, and it caused festering boils on humans and animals.

Scene 2

16:3 The second angel poured his bowl into the sea, and it became like the blood of a corpse, and every living thing in the sea died.

Upon what will the second angel pour his bowl? As the angel walks to the edge of the stage, before us is the great sea. It is the color of evil. The motion of the sea is hypnotic and takes us back in time to the beginning when it covered the earth. We have heard the stories of the monsters and beasts that live beneath the sea. The ancient ones believed seven-headed dragons fought against the all-powerful One for control of life itself. We remember what the prophet Isaiah has said:

"On that day the Lord with his cruel and great and strong sword will punish Leviathan the fleeing serpent, Leviathan the twisting serpent, and he will kill the dragon that is in the sea."[3]

"The second angel poured his bowl into the sea, and it became like the blood of a corpse, and every living thing in the sea died."

The audience began to shout.

"It is dead, we are delivered, the great and terrible beast is dead!"

The audience knows our Jewish ancestors believed the One fought with Leviathan and crushed his head. Here today, on this stage, the One has killed the dragon, the beast, and all that gave them birth, killed them with the blood of the saints. We believe that in the future the One will prevail over all evil. It is not the red dragon that has ultimate power, it is our God, our Creator, our Redeemer, our Rock, our Very Present Help in Time of Trouble. It is our God who is in control, no matter how strong and overwhelming the evil seems. In the end, my friend, the One will blot out evil from the earth and from the sea.

---

[3] Isaiah 27:1

Rev. 16:4–7

16:4 The third angel poured his bowl into the rivers and the springs of water, and they became blood.

16:5 And I heard the angel of the waters say, "You are just, O Holy One, who are and were, for you have judged these things;

16:6 because they shed the blood of saints and prophets, you have given them blood to drink. It is what they deserve!"

16:7 And I heard the altar respond, "Yes, O Lord God, the Almighty, your judgments are true and just!"

Scene 3

The scene has changed. The sea has become streams and rivers and springs bubbling up with beauty. Clear, clean water for animals and humans to use for drinking and bathing. The third angel, in this third scene, pours his bowl into these rivers and springs and they become blood. Now the empire has only blood to drink. This is the blood that is the wrath of God. It is the blood of Jews and Christians and all the innocents, shed by the empire, and saved in heaven to be poured out on the waters as a judgment. This is the blood upon which the empire will choke and one day die. It is the injustice and oppression and the violence that will one day gag the life out of the empire. Empires have gone to their death in times past; this empire will die of its own evil. Empires will die in the future from acting the part of God, and taking life that God has given.

And the angel of waters said,

> "You are just, O Holy One, who are and were, for you have judged these things; because they shed the blood of saints and prophets, you have given them blood to drink. It is what they deserve!"

My friend, join with the audience and with those martyred souls who have rested below the heavenly altar, and cry out,

"How long, O Lord, how long," and say, "Yes, O Lord God, the Almighty, your judgments are true and just!"

Scene 4

Scorching heat. Bright, white, blinding heat. Blasting heat comes from in front of the stage as the fourth scene begins. The audience covers their faces for protection. The sun has been placed in front of the stage.

Can you believe it, my friend, the sun, taken from the sky and put here in this theater?

"The fourth angel poured his bowl on the sun, and it was allowed to scorch them with fire; they were scorched by the fierce heat, but they cursed the name of God who had authority over these plagues, and they did not repent and give him glory."

There on the stage we can see the emperor Nero. What an exalted man he is. But he thinks he is not a man. He thinks he is Apollo, the sun god. So, god of the sun, if you are as powerful as you think, why don't you stop the sun from scorching us? If you are so exalted, why don't you put the sun back in the sky? You and other emperors like you who claim they are the sun god and have burned the Holy City to the ground, destroyed the temple of the One, murdered Jews and Christians, you think you have power over our God. You think you have power over the One who has created the earth, the moon and stars, and the sun.

The angel has now shown us who truly has the power. It is Yahweh, the God of Abraham, Isaac, and Jacob. It is Yahweh, the One, who put the sun in its place. Yahweh gives life, and by the grace of Yahweh are all people redeemed.

The sun god Nero and all the people who worship him will not believe. They still cling to the belief that the emperors are the ones who have the power and are gods. They torture themselves in this way.

16:8 The fourth angel poured his bowl on the sun, and it was allowed to scorch them with fire;

16:9 they were scorched by the fierce heat, but they cursed the name of God, who had authority over these plagues, and they did not repent and give him glory.

Rev. 16:10–11

16:10 The fifth angel poured his bowl on the throne of the beast, and its kingdom was plunged into darkness; people gnawed their tongues in agony,

16:11 and cursed the God of heaven because of their pains and sores, and they did not repent of their deeds.

Scene 5

"The fifth angel poured his bowl on the throne of the beast, and its kingdom was plunged into darkness; people gnawed their tongues in agony, and cursed the God of heaven because of their pains and sores and they did not repent of their deeds."

No one in the audience moved. This is not a darkness the audience can see. This is a darkness the audience can feel. This is a darkness the audience feels. This is a darkness we have been feeling our entire lives. It is the darkness of burning cities, burning bodies, burning fields and burning dreams. This is a darkness that penetrates human bones and takes away the capacity to hope, to plan, to build. It stifles joy, it smothers love, it stops the heart. This is the darkness that sits upon every throne, with every tyrant. It is the darkness of slavery, of oppression, and of legal violence. This is the darkness of past empires, of this empire, and of empires yet to come. In their souls the people live in constant unending agony, longing to see light, their pain so great they gnaw their tongues.

We do not blame the tyrant. We blame the God of heaven. We go on our way giving the tyrant power to suffocate and kill, and then cry out,

"Why, O God, does this happen?"

Do you believe, my friend the reader, that we can resist the tyrants? The people have, and have always had, and will always have the power to resist the tyrants. When we do not resist tyrants it is because to do so will bring us pain and death. When we resist it will be our blood that becomes the wrath of God which chokes the tyrant.

Scene 6

It is as cold now as it had been hot in the fourth scene. Everyone is wrapping up and some are trembling from the fear of what they see unfolding. The sixth angel is standing at the edge of the stage pouring his bowl over the side into the great river Euphrates. This pouring of the wrath of God dried up the great river, leaving no barrier between us and the kings from the east. Then on the stage appear together the red dragon empire, the beast emperor, and the second beast false prophet. Our anger at the evil of these three aberrations, our fear of being enslaved, our sadness at what they have done to our children causes us inconsolable shaking.

They open their mouths as though to speak, but instead of words there comes out of each of them the evil demon of Persia, the frog of death.[4] This frog, like the kings of the earth it is sent to find, leads people to their death. They know each other well, for both kings and frogs cannot stop their work until someone dies. These evil frogs lead the kings and their armies to the place called Armageddon, where they are joined by the red dragon, the beast, and the second beast to wait for the coming of the army of God. What a scene this is! You cannot imagine an army this large. The number of soldiers so vast they can't be counted. The red dragon empire is there in front of them all, waiting to fight the army of God.

The audience thought this day would never come. Some have already left for home. We have seen the signs of this day of the great battle all through this play, but it has never yet taken place. Each time the battle failed to happen, we were promised that the day would come when the battle would take place between the kings of the earth and the army of God. We were told it would come like a thief in the night. We were warned to be ready, lest we be found naked in body or spirit.

Is this it? Is this the scene for which we have waited the entire play? The scene in which the empire is destroyed by the violence it deserves, by the violence that has given the empire life, the violence it has inflicted on the people within its borders and without? Is this blood of the martyrs, the blood which is the wrath of God, finally going to choke the empire, and all the empires of the earth, to death?

---

[4] The Encyclopedia Of Religion, Vol. 5 (New York: MacMillan Publishing Company, 1987) p. 443.

Rev. 16:12–16

16:12 The sixth angel poured his bowl on the great river Euphrates, and its water was dried up in order to prepare the way for the kings from the east.

16:13 And I saw three foul spirits like frogs coming from the mouth of the dragon, from the mouth of the beast, and from the mouth of the false prophet.

16:14 These are demonic spirits, performing signs, who go abroad to the kings of the whole world, to assemble them for battle on the great day of God the Almighty.

16:15 ("See, I am coming like a thief! Blessed is the one who stays awake and is clothed, not going about naked and exposed to shame.")

16:16 And they assembled them at the place that in Hebrew is called Harmagedon.

Rev. 16:17–21

16:17 The seventh angel poured his bowl into the air, and a loud voice came out of the temple, from the throne, saying, "It is done!"

16:18 And there came flashes of lightning, rumblings, peals of thunder, and a violent earthquake, such as had not occurred since people were upon the earth, so violent was that earthquake.

16:19 The great city was split into three parts, and the cities of the nations fell. God remembered great Babylon and gave her the wine-cup of the fury of his wrath.

16:20 And every island fled away, and no mountains were to be found;

16:21 and huge hailstones, each weighing about a hundred pounds, dropped from heaven on people, until they cursed God for the plague of the hail, so fearful was that plague.

Scene 7

In this seventh scene, the seventh angel pours his bowl into the air. It is all that can be scraped together of what is left of the wrath of God. There are flashes of lightning, rumblings, peals of thunder, and a violent earthquake, the greatest earthquake in the history of the earth.

The audience knows that the One is present, and we know what form the earthquake takes. The earthquake is the very winepress of the wrath of God. The earthquake has been pressing and shaking the life out of believers for a very long time. The earthquake is caused by the rhythm of the empire's unstoppable marching army.

As a result of this earthquake, the great city of Jerusalem is split into three parts. We recognize these three parts, don't we, my friend? Jews who have been left in Judah after the fall of Jerusalem. Jews who have been sent or driven to all parts of the empire. Those who call themselves Christians. It is not just Jerusalem that has fallen at this quaking of the earth. At this marching of the army of the empire, all the cities of all the nations fall.

Babylon, that evil god worshiped as Roma, will not be left out of judgment. Roma will soon drink the wine-cup of the fury of God's wrath! When this day comes, nothing can save the empire. It is going to be destroyed. The islands of the oceans will scream their independence, and that scream will be heard and repeated from the side of every mountain along the empire's frontier. And God will send hailstones on the empire, as the empire has sent a hail of stones upon the heads of all the cities it has destroyed and conquered for hundreds of years.

Then a loud voice, the very voice of God, comes out of the temple, from the throne, saying,

"It is done!"

This is the very last of the wrath of God. There is no more. There will be no more. There can be no more. God's wrath is ended, as it was promised in the last scene of act four. How can this be? How do these last seven scenes add up to all that is left of the wrath of God while the great army of the kings of the earth still stands ready to do battle at the place called Armageddon? If there is no more wrath of God, what will happen with this army? How will we have our vengeance?

Here Ends the Fifth Act

Rev. 18:1–3 & 24

18:1 After this I saw another angel coming down from heaven, having great authority; and the earth was made bright with his splendor.

18:2 He called out with a mighty voice, Fallen, fallen is Babylon the great! It has become a dwelling place of demons, a haunt of every foul and hateful bird, a haunt of every foul and hateful beast.

18:3 For all the nations have drunk of the wine of the wrath of her fornication, and the kings of the earth have committed fornication with her, and the merchants of the earth have grown rich from the power of her luxury."

18:24 And in you was found the blood of prophets and of saints, and of all who have been slaughtered on earth."

Future Times

In future times,
In the dark times that are to come,
When cities are no longer cities but have become
    something else.
In the cool of the night,
As you sit around your fire,
Your child will say:
"Tell us of cities,
Tell us of women, beautiful and elegant,
Of men rich and powerful.
Tell us of tall buildings,
Nice restaurants,
Theaters.
Tell us of big houses, elevators, and trains that went from
    place to place."

It is then you must tell the truth.
Remember the way it was in former days.

Start at the beginning,
With the stories of the ancient ones.

Cain killed his brother, then built a city.
Nimrod received the curse,
And built Nineveh, that evil city,
Constructed by a warrior.

God came to earth one day. Saw the city with its wall and
    tower.
Saw the power that city gave a few to inflict suffering on the
    many,
On those who dwell in tents.
God said, "This is not the way I had meant for things to be."
The city dwellers were given different languages.
They could not talk to each other.
God sent them away from their city and their place,
So they could not talk with God.

The ancient people did evil in the sight of God,
And again they built their cities.
They built Sodom and Gomorrah.
No cities were ever so violent as those.
To rape and rape and rape again until their guests were
    dead.
Strangers in their land.
People who did not know their danger when they entered
    the city.
They did it to the vulnerable,
So they did it to God.

A man of power needed a house to hold his gold.
Raamses and Pithom, the treasure cities, were built
To hold gold and silver and precious things.
The people built them for the pharaoh,
Were forced to build them.
They were slaves.

You will have said all you need to say of cities.
The ancient people built their walls,
And to each other could not talk.
When they could not talk with each other,
They could not talk with God.

Their cities had a sickness.
The sickness of violence.
Violence that murdered and raped.
A madness of such proportions it is remembered still.

And when a strong one begins to accumulate gold,
God on gold,
The people are enslaved.
They have to work, to love, to die as slaves.
When the strong ones become rich, the people become
    slaves.

It is what you must tell your child
In future times,
In the dark times that are to come.
When cities are no longer cities but have become something
    else.
As you sit in the cool of the night,
Around your fire.
To warn them,
To teach them,
The curse of building walls.

Act VI

Rev. 17:1–20:3

The Setting

We all sit in the theater pondering what we have just seen. Seven bowls poured down upon the earth by seven angels. We heard the loud voice from heaven, the voice of the One who cried out, "It is done," for with these seven bowls "the wrath of God is ended." Our question is, "How can this be the end of the wrath of God?" Those kings from the east have crossed the great river Euphrates and are left waiting at the place called Armageddon with the three beasts of the Roman empire. The throne of the empire has been cast in darkness, a darkness one did not have to see, but rather feel. The sores, the bloody ocean, the bloody water, the scorching sun, and the plague of hail, are they still going on behind the curtain? For what are we all waiting? Is God going to bring this play to an end with justice? Are we to get our vengeance, or is God not finished redeeming the empire with our blood?

We watch on the stage as one of the seven angels who poured one of the seven bowls said to us,

> "Come, I will show you the judgment of the great whore who is seated on many waters, with whom the kings of the earth have committed fornication, and with the wine of whose fornication the inhabitants of the earth have become drunk."

Rev. 17:1–2

17:1 Then one of the seven angels who had the seven bowls came and said to me, "Come, I will show you the judgment of the great whore who is seated on many waters,

17:2 with whom the kings of the earth have committed fornication, and with the wine of whose fornication the inhabitants of the earth have become drunk."

Rev. 17:3–5

17:3 So he carried me away in the spirit into a wilderness, and I saw a woman sitting on a scarlet beast that was full of blasphemous names, and it had seven heads and ten horns.

17:4 The woman was clothed in purple and scarlet, and adorned with gold and jewels and pearls, holding in her hand a golden cup full of abominations and the impurities of her fornication;

17:5 and on her forehead was written a name, a mystery: "Babylon the great, mother of whores and of earth's abominations."

Scene I

In the spirit, an angel carries us away into a wilderness. Is this the wilderness of Sinai where the people rebelled against Moses and threw their gold into the fire, then out popped a golden calf?[1] Or is this the wilderness where our Lord was tried and tempted?[2]

In the wilderness we see a woman sitting on a scarlet beast. My friend, those of us who have lived under the Roman empire know this to be a city called Woman. She is the daughter of the murderer Cain.[3] The child of Nimrod who had received the curse from Noah and was the first warrior.[4] She is called Babel, for she has made a name for herself on the earth.[5] Her violence knows no bounds, and we remember her as Sodom and Gomorrah.[6] She enslaved our people when her name was Pithom and Rameses.[7] We learned from her to put our trust in God, not in walls, when her name was Jericho.[8] We would live to regret the power she gave the one we called King. How glorious she appeared to us with our temple in her midst.

But she deceived us, and the One called out from heaven,

"I will hide my eyes from you; even if you offer many prayers, I will not listen. Your hands are full of blood; wash and make yourselves clean. Take your evil deeds out of my sight! Stop doing wrong, learn to do right! Seek justice, encourage the oppressed. Defend the cause of the fatherless, plead the case of the widow. . . . See how the faithful city has become a harlot! She once was full of justice; righteousness used to dwell in her—but now murderers! Your silver has become dross, your choice wine is diluted with water. Your rulers are rebels, companions of thieves; they all love bribes and chase after gifts. They do not defend the cause of the fatherless; the widow's case does not come before them."[9]

---

[1] Exodus 32:21–24
[2] Mark 1:12–13
[3] Genesis 4:17
[4] Genesis 10:8–11
[5] Genesis 11:9
[6] Genesis 19:1–11
[7] Exodus 1:8–14
[8] Joshua 6:1–21
[9] Isaiah 1:15–23

She was our slave master Asshur,[10] and the evil one called Babylon.[11] She was called Susa,[12] then her name was changed to Rome. We know this woman. We remember her. We suffer now from the pain of her evil.

But look at her upon that stage! With all that beauty, how can she be evil? She wears the royal purple and scarlet; she is adorned with gold and jewels and pearls. How can we not bow before her?

We do not bow, for she holds in her hand the cup of our suffering. The golden cup full of the blood of those who believed. The cup of abominations she filled at the destruction of our temple and the slaughter of the Christians in her midst. We cannot bow, for on her forehead is written a name, a mystery.

"Babylon the great, mother of whores and of earth's abominations."

She is seated on the scarlet beast with seven heads and ten horns, the beast we all know. The beast we all fear. The beast that gives the woman her power.

Rev. 17:3–5

17:3 So he carried me away in the spirit into a wilderness, and I saw a woman sitting on a scarlet beast that was full of blasphemous names, and it had seven heads and ten horns.

17:4 The woman was clothed in purple and scarlet, and adorned with gold and jewels and pearls, holding in her hand a golden cup full of abominations and the impurities of her fornication;

17:5 and on her forehead was written a name, a mystery: "Babylon the great, mother of whores and of earth's abominations."

---

[10]Capital of Assyria
[11]Capital of Babylonia
[12] Capital of Persia

Rev. 17:6–18

17:6 And I saw that the woman was drunk with the blood of the saints and the blood of the witnesses to Jesus. When I saw her, I was greatly amazed.

17:7 But the angel said to me, "Why are you so amazed? I will tell you the mystery of the woman, and of the beast with seven heads and ten horns that carries her.

17:8 The beast that you saw was, and is not, and is about to ascend from the bottomless pit and go to destruction. And the inhabitants of the earth, whose names have not been written in the book of life from the foundation of the world, will be amazed when they see the beast, because it was and is not and is to come.

17:9 "This calls for a mind that has wisdom: the seven heads are seven mountains on which the woman is seated; also, they are seven kings,

17:10 of whom five have fallen, one is living, and the other has not yet come; and when he comes, he must remain only a little while.

17:11 As for the beast that was and is not, it is an eighth but it belongs to the seven, and it goes to destruction.

17:12 And the ten horns that you saw are ten kings who have not yet received a kingdom, but they are to receive authority as kings for one hour, together with the beast.

17:13 These are united in yielding their power and authority to the beast;

Scene 2

It is obvious to the audience that the woman is drunk. She is drunk with the blood from the golden cup in scene one.

The audience recognized the cup as the cup Christ chose to drink in the Garden. We know it is the cup that was filled with the blood of the saints when the temple was destroyed by Rome and human lives were sacrificed to the god Roma. It is the cup filled by the river of legions that has come out of the dragon's mouth to drown the followers of Christ. It is this cup of death that makes this mother of whores think she is all-powerful and invincible. It is this cup that will lead to her end. She will choke on her power. She cannot oppress forever. One day she must pay the price of the oppressor.

The angel is explaining the meaning of the scarlet beast upon which the great woman sits, but the audience does not need much explanation. This is the beast I have told you about, my friend, in other scenes of this play, and we have become most familiar from encountering this beast each day as we go about our business.

"The beast that you saw was, and is not, and is about to ascend from the bottomless pit and go to destruction."

This scarlet beast *was*—from before our grandfathers, from the days of the Republic. Yet before the Republic named this beast, it had other names: Persia, Babylonia, Assyria, Egypt.

This scarlet beast *is not*—this beast thinks itself a god. It calls its emperor the son of god and builds idols in his likeness. The city of Rome that gives life to the beast is called Roma the god, the mother god. It is from this beast that the emperor gets his power and throne. The audience is hissing now. They begin to chant,

"No! No! No! This beast is not a god!"

This scarlet beast is about to ascend from the bottomless pit and go to destruction—we saw this beast come from the bottomless pit along with the beast from the sea and the beast from the land. It is still coming from that pit which is Rome. They sent out the frogs to gather the kings from the east. The beast is coming from the pit with all of its soldiers, with all of its horses, with all of its machines of war. The beast is waiting even now at Armageddon for the day when the heavenly army will come to destroy it.

But the people are amazed at this beast. It has wielded its power for so long they think it is a god. It stands ready, two hundred million strong, waiting at Armageddon. People who do not share a name recorded in the book of life are amazed at the beast.

The angel is calling us to understand. The angel continues to explain who the beast is. The seven heads of the beast are the seven mountains upon which the woman sits. The seven heads represent the complete number of the kings who call themselves gods. Like the kings who call themselves god, the empire itself, the scarlet beast, scarlet from the blood of the saints, considers itself a god and will go to destruction with the seven kings.

The ten horns of the beast are ten kings who have yielded their power and authority to the beast, and now stand at Armageddon, waiting

"to make war on the Lamb, and the Lamb will conquer them, for he is Lord of lords and King of kings, and those with him are called and chosen and faithful."

These kings came from the east and have no kingdom here, but they will battle the heavenly army for one hour together with the beast.

This evil woman, the city of Rome, sits on many waters. These waters are the voice of the Son of Man, for when he spoke his voice sounded like many waters. These waters are the legions that flowed from the mouth of the red dragon. These waters are the people, the multitudes and nations and languages. These are the people the great whore has subjugated for so long. These are the people who give this evil woman her food and all that makes her strong. The kings from the east, those ten horns, join with the beast in consuming the woman. They sap her of her wealth, her strength, her very life. They have done the will of God by giving their armies and their kingdoms to the beast, until they meet the heavenly army at Armageddon. The beast has burned her with fire to make room for his palaces, and then blamed the Christians.

"The woman is the great city that rules over the kings of the earth."

Rev. 17:14–18

17:14 they will make war on the Lamb, and the Lamb will conquer them, for he is Lord of lords and King of kings, and those with him are called and chosen and faithful."

17:15 And he said to me, "The waters that you saw, where the whore is seated, are peoples and multitudes and nations and languages.

17:16 And the ten horns that you saw, they and the beast will hate the whore; they will make her desolate and naked; they will devour her flesh and burn her up with fire.

17:17 For God has put it into their hearts to carry out his purpose by agreeing to give their kingdom to the beast, until the words of God will be fulfilled.

17:18 The woman you saw is the great city that rules over the kings of the earth."

Rev. 18:1–19:10

18:1 After this I saw another angel coming down from heaven, having great authority; and the earth was made bright with his splendor.

18:2 He called out with a mighty voice, Fallen, fallen is Babylon the great! It has become a dwelling place of demons, a haunt of every foul and hateful bird, a haunt of every foul and hateful beast.

18:3 For all the nations have drunk of the wine of the wrath of her fornication, and the kings of the earth have committed fornication with her, and the merchants of the earth have grown rich from the power of her luxury."

18:4 Then I heard another voice from heaven saying, Come out of her, my people, so that you do not take part in her sins, and so that you do not share in her plagues;

18:5 for her sins are heaped high as heaven, and God has remembered her iniquities.

18:6 Render to her as she herself has rendered, and repay her double for her deeds; mix a double draught for her in the cup she mixed.

18:7 As she glorified herself and lived luxuriously, so give her a like measure of torment and grief. Since in her heart she says, I rule as a queen; I am no widow, and I will never see grief,'

18:8 therefore her plagues will come in a single day—pestilence and mourning and famine—and she will be burned with fire; for mighty is the Lord God who judges her."

Scene 3

The audience is on their feet applauding the beginning of this third scene.

There is an angel I wish you could see, who lights up the theater with his splendor, coming down from heaven and calling out, "Fallen, fallen is Babylon the great!" We have heard this before, but this time we feel it is going to happen. The people are ecstatic. We have been waiting for the empire to get what it has coming. We thought it was going to happen with the great earthquake in scene six of act two, but the angels were not allowed to let the four winds go. The One was not finished redeeming the empire.

We thought the empire was going to get what it had coming when the angel blew the sixth trumpet. But an angel, like this one, came and stopped the two hundred million of God's cavalry, and told John to eat the little scroll. After he ate the scroll we all knew the idea of the empire's destruction was a mistake. The One was not finished redeeming the empire.

We thought the day of the Lord had come in the sixth scene of act four when the great ingathering of believers took place, but the empire was not judged for the One had not finished redeeming the empire. In scene six of the fifth act we were ready for the day of the great battle when the kings of the east, who gave their allegiance to the three beasts of the empire at Armageddon, joined with the beasts for the coming of the heavenly hosts. But it did not happen; they wait there still.

Now we know the empire will crumble, for the great city that gave life and wealth to the empire by the power of her luxury, Babylon, is fallen. It has happened. It has become a dwelling place for all the foreign gods of all the countries the empire has conquered. It has become a haunt of every foul and hateful bird, birds that have eaten the bodies of the fallen, a haunt of every foul and hateful beast, beasts that tore apart our families in the hippodromes. She, that great city, has fallen because all the nations have been forced to drink their own blood shed by the wrath of this god who is not a god, Roma.

The theater quiets.

"Another voice from heaven is saying, 'Come out of her, my people, so that you do not take part in her sins, and so that you do not share in her plagues.'"

The One never stops redeeming. The One is calling out those who will believe, those called by the names "believer" and "faithful one," names that have been recorded in the book of life since time began. The One calls to those who repent of the sins of violence, death and idolatrous wealth

"that are heaped high as heaven."

These are the iniquities from which Roma has not repented, so the One still remembers.

Many people begin answering the voice from heaven,

"Render to her as she herself has rendered, and repay her double for her deeds; mix a double draught for her in the cup she mixed."
"Match her golden palaces and luxurious living with a like measure of the torment and grief she has used to oppress."
"For so long she said in her heart, 'I rule as a queen; I am no widow, and I will never see grief.'"

She has been blind. She refused to see the grief of slavery, the enslavement of many nations, the carrying away of people to slavery and death. Now this blindness has come to destroy her. In a single day she will share what the people have always known: disease, mourning, and famine. Those kings of the east will join with the beast emperors and burn her with fire, for it is the mighty Lord God who sentences her to suffer the pain of her own sins, to drink the cup of blood she has shed.

Those kings that have committed fornication with her by sharing in her great wealth,

"They will weep and wail over her when they see the smoke of her burning; they will stand far off, in fear of her torment, and say, 'Alas, alas, the great city, Babylon, the mighty city! For in one hour your judgment has come.'"

Rev. 18:9–18:16

18:9 And the kings of the earth, who committed fornication and lived in luxury with her, will weep and wail over her when they see the smoke of her burning;

18:10 they will stand far off, in fear of her torment, and say, Alas, alas, the great city, Babylon, the mighty city! For in one hour your judgment has come."

18:11 And the merchants of the earth weep and mourn for her, since no one buys their cargo anymore,

18:12 cargo of gold, silver, jewels and pearls, fine linen, purple, silk and scarlet, all kinds of scented wood, all articles of ivory, all articles of costly wood, bronze, iron, and marble,

18:13 cinnamon, spice, incense, myrrh, frankincense, wine, olive oil, choice flour and wheat, cattle and sheep, horses and chariots, slaves —and human lives.

18:14 "The fruit for which your soul longed has gone from you, and all your dainties and your splendor are lost to you, never to be found again!"

18:15 The merchants of these wares, who gained wealth from her, will stand far off, in fear of her torment, weeping and mourning aloud,

18:16 "Alas, alas, the great city, clothed in fine linen, in purple and scarlet, adorned with gold, with jewels, and with pearls!

Rev. 18:17–23

18:17 For in one hour all this wealth has been laid waste!" And all shipmasters and seafarers, sailors and all whose trade is on the sea, stood far off

18:18 and cried out as they saw the smoke of her burning, What city was like the great city?"

18:19 And they threw dust on their heads, as they wept and mourned, crying out, Alas, alas, the great city, where all who had ships at sea grew rich by her wealth! For in one hour she has been laid waste.

18:20 Rejoice over her, O heaven, you saints and apostles and prophets! For God has given judgment for you against her."

18:21 Then a mighty angel took up a stone like a great millstone and threw it into the sea, saying, With such violence Babylon the great city will be thrown down, and will be found no more;

18:22 and the sound of harpists and minstrels and of flutists and trumpeters will be heard in you no more; and an artisan of any trade will be found in you no more; and the sound of the millstone will be heard in you no more;

18:23 and the light of a lamp will shine in you no more; and the voice of bridegroom and bride will be heard in you no more; for your merchants were the magnates of the earth, and all nations were deceived by your sorcery.

It is not just the kings who commit fornication with this city Babylon. The merchants also get rich off the labor of her slaves. The woman clothed in purple and scarlet, and adorned with gold and jewels and pearls, would not have this wealth if she had not enslaved our people. Slaves who work the mines, oar the ships, harvest the grapes on the great estates. Slaves who live in hovels and watch their babies die. The empire's slaves are the source of the merchants' wealth which they carried to the city, where it is worshiped as the truly greatest god.

Willingly did the merchants commit this fornication with the god Roma. They brought her

"gold, silver, jewels and pearls, fine linen, purple, silk and scarlet, all kinds of scented wood, all articles of ivory, all articles of costly wood, bronze, iron, and marble, cinnamon, spice, incense, myrrh, frankincense, wine, olive oil, choice flour and wheat, cattle and sheep, horses and chariots, slaves—that is, human souls."

The audience is outraged at the list of idolatrous wealth and begins to throw things at the woman on the stage. Some in the audience are slaves, and most of us are related to slaves. Of all the commodities bought and sold, human souls are listed last. This is the empire's greatest sin. This turning of human life into an expendable commodity and giving it a value less than that of choice flour or sheep is the iniquity above all others that is remembered by the One. This is the iniquity that will serve to destroy the empire.

"Merchants from all the earth weep and mourn for her, since no one buys their cargo anymore!"

The merchants stand far off and the audience can see how sad they are to watch their demon god of wealth destroyed, but they do nothing to help. They feel powerless. The merchants fear that this torment of the city will be turned on them, and they weep and mourn aloud,

"Alas, alas, the great city, clothed in fine linen, in purple and scarlet, adorned with gold, with jewels, and with pearls! For in one hour all this wealth has been laid waste!"

The audience cheers as the angel points to the woman and says,

"The fruit for which your soul longed has gone from you, and all your dainties and your splendor are lost to you, never to be found again!"

Now it is the shipmasters' and seafarers' turn to mourn. Standing in their ships on stage opposite the great city, they watch it burn. How sad they are that they no longer have a port to buy all they can collect.

"They threw dust on their heads as they wept and mourned, crying out, 'Alas, alas, the great city, where all who had ships at sea grew rich by her wealth!'"

Wealth is her greatest idolatry.

As the kings, merchants and shipmasters stood and cried for their loss, the Jews and Christians whose souls have waited in heaven are told by the angel,

"Rejoice over her, O heaven, you saints and apostles and prophets! For God has given judgment for you against her."

These are the souls under the altar who have waited so long for justice to be done. It was their lives the empire took, while she played at being a god. These are the tens of thousands of Jews killed when Jerusalem was destroyed.

These are the Christians burned to death after the emperor Nero had burned the city. That fire has never been extinguished in the hearts of the oppressed, and it is now rekindled against the oppressor.

Now a mighty angel comes onto the stage, lifts a great millstone and throws it into the sea.

The audience hopes this stone weighs as much as all the stones that have been thrown upon all the cities, crushing the life out of all the people subjugated by the empire. Her own actions have brought her end.

"Let anyone who has an ear listen: if you kill with the sword, with the sword you must be killed."[13]

---

[13] Rev. 13:9 & 10b

Rev. 18:24–19:8

18:24 And in you was found the blood of prophets and of saints, and of all who have been slaughtered on earth."

19:1 After this I heard what seemed to be the loud voice of a great multitude in heaven, saying, Hallelujah! Salvation and glory and power to our God,

19:2 for his judgments are true and just; he has judged the great whore who corrupted the earth with her fornication, and he has avenged on her the blood of his servants."

19:3 Once more they said, Hallelujah! The smoke goes up from her forever and ever."

19:4 And the twenty-four elders and the four living creatures fell down and worshiped God who is seated on the throne, saying, Amen. Hallelujah!"

19:5 And from the throne came a voice saying, Praise our God, all you his servants, and all who fear him, small and great."

19:6 Then I heard what seemed to be the voice of a great multitude, like the sound of many waters and like the sound of mighty thunderpeals, crying out, Hallelujah! For the Lord our God the Almighty reigns.

19:7 Let us rejoice and exult and give him the glory, for the marriage of the Lamb has come, and his bride has made herself ready;

19:8 to her it has been granted to be clothed with fine linen, bright and pure"— for the fine linen is the righteous deeds of the saints.

Rev. 19:9–19:10

19:9 And the angel said to me, "Write this: Blessed are those who are invited to the marriage supper of the Lamb." And he said to me, "These are true words of God."

19:10 Then I fell down at his feet to worship him, but he said to me, "You must not do that! I am a fellow servant with you and your comrades who hold the testimony of Jesus. Worship God! For the testimony of Jesus is the spirit of prophecy."

The mighty angel proclaims,

"With such violence Babylon the great city will be thrown down, and will be found no more; and the sound of harpists and minstrels and of flutists and trumpeters will be heard in you no more; and an artisan of any trade will be found in you no more; and the sound of the millstone will be heard in you no more; and the light of a lamp will shine in you no more; and the voice of bridegroom and bride will be heard in you no more; for your merchants were the magnates of the earth, and all nations were deceived by your sorcery. And in you was found the blood of prophets and of saints, and of all who have been slaughtered on earth."

We now understand why the One has not punished the empire before this. The punishment does not come from the One. The punishment, which is the wrath of God, comes from the deeds of the city turned in upon itself. It is the greed and violence by which it lived, eating away at the life of the empire like a consuming disease that will bring about the end. Still we hear the words of the angel,

"Come out of her, my people, so that you do not share in her plagues."

The One wills that not one soul should die, but that all would be brought to repentance.

The theater is filled with music.

"A great multitude in heaven, saying, 'Hallelujah! Salvation and glory and power to our God, for his judgments are true and just; he has judged the great whore who corrupted the earth with her fornication, and he has avenged on her the blood of his servants.'"

The twenty-four elders and the four creatures appear and fall down and worship the One who is seated on the throne, saying,

"Amen. Halleluhah!"

Then a choir so large it could not be numbered calls us all to the feast of the marriage of the Lamb.

"Hallelujah! For the Lord our God the Almighty reigns. Let us rejoice and exult and give him the glory, for the marriage of the Lamb has come, and his bride has made herself ready; to her it has been granted to be clothed with fine linen, bright and pure—for the fine linen is the righteous deeds of the saints."

"Blessed are those who are invited to the marriage supper of the Lamb."

The audience is going crazy.

"Yes," they are shouting, "we will come! Yes, we want to be invited no matter what the cost! Yes, we want the Lamb united with his glorious bride, the church! The bride of the Lamb who is far more radiant than the great whore. The bride of the Lamb whose righteous deeds outshine the most dazzling wealth of the city of Rome. Yes, we want the marriage supper of the Lamb to be held today!"

John fell at the feet of this Jewish angel on the stage, but the angel tells him not to do that for he is a

"fellow servant with you and your comrades who hold the testimony of Jesus. Worship God! For the testimony of Jesus is the spirit of prophecy."

It is not meant for Christians and Jews to be divided, for the testimony of Jesus has at its core the power and potency of the Jewish prophets.

Rev. 19:11–16

19:11 Then I saw heaven opened, and there was a white horse! Its rider is called Faithful and True, and in righteousness he judges and makes war.

19:12 His eyes are like a flame of fire, and on his head are many diadems; and he has a name inscribed that no one knows but himself.

Scene 4

Do you remember the white horse and its rider of the first seal? Now heaven is open and we see that white horse whose rider has the bow of the clouds. Remember, he came out conquering and to conquer. The audience is yelling and screaming as scene four begins, because following him on white horses are the armies of heaven wearing fine linen, white and pure. Now will be the great battle we have all been waiting for, when the armies of heaven meet the armies of the red dragon and the two beasts as well as the kings from the east who stand ready at Armageddon. Now we are sure the one who is to conquer will prevail over the beast from the bottomless pit.

This One on the white horse John calls Faithful and True. No matter how long it takes or how cut off we feel, the deliverer will come. The deliverer is faithful to the words of the prophets who say he will come. The deliverer is true to his agreement that he will not abandon the believers with whom the covenant has been made. His eyes are the same eyes we see in the setting of act one, "like a flame of fire." We saw at the beginning, when time was young and the first seal broken, the rider of the white horse was given a crown. Now on his head are many diadems, more diadems than worn by the emperor beast he has come to conquer.

"He has a name inscribed that no one knows but himself."

We have searched since the time of Moses for that word that would name God, that would describe and define God.

We have yet to find just the right word. Moses used the words, I Am.[14] Others have used the words: Jealous,[15] the Almighty,[16] Most High,[17] Everlasting,[18] Rock,[19] Shepherd,[20] Ancient of Days,[21] First and Last.[22] We search for the word that will possess God's power and essence. Now, here before this audience *is the word!*

"And his name is called the Word of God."

This one on the white horse is that person who describes and defines God, who possesses God's power and essence.

"From his mouth comes a sharp sword with which to strike down the nations, and he will rule them with a rod of iron."

Yes, this is the God we have been waiting for, decisive and ready to do battle. He has a scepter made of iron. He will be a strong king, for he has iron. But we do not see the sword. In the audience we search each other's faces for an explanation. Where is the sword? We do not see this sword he will use to strike down the nations.

"He is clothed in a robe dipped in blood."

There is his own blood from his crucifixion. The Romans killed him, as they have slaughtered so many others in the empire. The blood of all who have died is there. He has been present in the winepress that has produced this blood upon which the empire will choke, this blood that makes the empire drunk with power and crazy in the head. This drunken power will lead them the way of a drunken man: poor, dejected and lying stuporous in his burning house. This blood, produced by legal and illegal violence, is the anger of God. Letting people suffer the consequences of their actions is the wrath of God. Now this One who is Faith-

Rev. 19:13–16

19:13 He is clothed in a robe dipped in blood, and his name is called The Word of God.

19:14 And the armies of heaven, wearing fine linen, white and pure, were following him on white horses.

19:15 From his mouth comes a sharp sword with which to strike down the nations, and he will rule them with a rod of iron; he will tread the wine press of the fury of the wrath of God the Almighty.

19:16 On his robe and on his thigh he has a name inscribed, "King of kings and Lord of lords."

---

[14] Exodus 3:14
[15] Exodus 34:14
[16] Genesis 17:1
[17] Genesis 14:18
[18] Genesis 21:33
[19] Deuteronomy 32:4
[20] Genesis 49:24
[21] Daniel 7:22
[22] Isaiah 48:12

ful and True will use this Roman-built winepress against the Romans themselves. The Word of God will tread this winepress and squash the life out of the Romans, for it is in righteousness he judges and makes war. The audience is on their feet. We are screaming approval. This is what we have been waiting for. We want to see this happen!

> "On his robe and on his thigh he has a name inscribed, 'King of kings and Lord of lords.'"

There is no other as great as Christ. The dragon and the two beasts who are the empire, the emperor, and the proconsul priests of Rome, with all the kings of the east that the frogs had recruited to come to their death, are no match for the one on the white horse leading the heavenly hosts.

Scene 5

We all cover our eyes for now the stage is again flooded with light. Because it is so bright, we can barely see an angel

"standing in the sun. With a loud voice he called to all the birds that fly in midheaven, 'Come, gather for the great supper of God, to eat the flesh of kings, the flesh of captains, the flesh of the mighty, the flesh of horses and their riders— flesh of all, both free and slave, both small and great."

Yes, birds, come and feast. While you are eating the flesh of kings, we will be celebrating the feast of the Lamb and his bride that the angel told us about in scene three. After all believers have been redeemed, there will be a great marriage supper of the Lamb and his bride the church. A great marriage celebration between the Lamb and all who believe. I tell you, my friend, those who have oppressed, those who have stolen freedom and faith and land and gold and life itself, they, and all soldiers and slaves who have served the bloody red dragon willingly, will be feasted upon by the fowl of heaven.

Rev. 19:17–18

19:17 Then I saw an angel standing in the sun, and with a loud voice he called to all the birds that fly in midheaven, "Come, gather for the great supper of God,

19:18 to eat the flesh of kings, the flesh of captains, the flesh of the mighty, the flesh of horses and their riders —flesh of all, both free and slave, both small and great."

Rev. 19:19–21

19:19 Then I saw the beast and the kings of the earth with their armies gathered to make war against the rider on the horse and against his army.

19:20 And the beast was captured, and with it the false prophet who had performed in its presence the signs by which he deceived those who had received the mark of the beast and those who worshiped its image. These two were thrown alive into the lake of fire that burns with sulfur.

19:21 And the rest were killed by the sword of the rider on the horse, the sword that came from his mouth; and all the birds were gorged with their flesh.

Scene 6

Have you observed in this play that the sixth scene has always been where it seemed the great battle or judgment of the empire would take place? Yet in each act the audience has been robbed of what we have come to see. There is a lot of grumbling in the theater now because here we are at the sixth scene. We want the empire to be destroyed, but we are skeptical.

Now is when the One Faithful and True, the Word of God, riding on his white horse followed by the mighty hosts of heaven, needs to wipe out the empire. Here, now, is where the Word of God needs to put the empire in the very winepress they have built for the believers, and squash them. Let their blood flow as high as a horse's bridle, for two hundred miles, as they did to the believers in scene six of act four. Here, now, the King of kings and Lord of lords needs to take his sharp sword and cut down and kill this destroyer-emperor-satan, and all who serve him: the entire red dragon-empire, and especially those who enforce its laws; the second beast-proconsul-priests; and along with them all the kings from the east and their armies.

And there they stand waiting, where they have stood since the sixth scene of act five: the three beasts and all who serve them, the kings from the east and all who serve them, two hundred million strong. Waiting to join battle with the heavenly hosts on the white horses. What a great battle this will be!

> "And the [emperor] beast was captured, and with it the false prophet [proconsul] who had performed in its presence the signs by which he deceived those who had received the mark of the beast and those who worshiped its image. These two were thrown alive into the lake of fire that burns with sulfur. The rest were killed by the sword of the rider on the horse, the sword that came from his mouth."

The audience looks at each other.

"What happened?" they ask. "Where was the great battle?"

It was all over in the blinking of an eye. The emperor and his governor priests where thrown into the lake of fire. We want to stand and cheer, we want to shout, "Hallelujah, praise Yahweh," but there was no great battle?

The Word of God simply spoke to the rest of the two hundred million, and they fell to the ground. And what did he say to them? Some think he said, "Be dead!" Some think he said, "I slay you!"

"No," shouted someone near the front, "What he said was, 'I love you!'"

The Word of God, the One who is Faithful and True, the One who makes war and judges in righteousness, did not put them in the winepress at all. He redeemed them! The great battle at Armageddon was no battle at all. It was a sermon, a great act of redemption!

Rev. 20:1–3

20:1 Then I saw an angel coming down from heaven, holding in his hand the key to the bottomless pit and a great chain.

20:2 He seized the dragon, that ancient serpent, who is the Devil and Satan, and bound him for a thousand years,

20:3 and threw him into the pit, and locked and sealed it over him, so that he would deceive the nations no more, until the thousand years were ended. After that he must be let out for a little while.

Scene 7

Hoots and raspberries, pointed fingers, gestures of an "unChristian nature" are coming from the audience. In this seventh scene, an angel has come down from heaven who holds the key that can lock the bottomless pit.

"He seized the dragon, that ancient serpent, who is the Devil and Satan, and bound him for a thousand years, and threw him into the pit, and locked and sealed it over him, so that he would deceive the nations no more, until the thousand years were ended."

Well, my friend, finally the empire, that ancient serpent, gets what it has coming. It deserves to die, to be locked away. It should receive double for all its sins. How can it be possible for this empire to receive double, for its sins are so great? How many thousands no, tens of thousands, has it crucified for being enemies of the state? How many millions has it enslaved for the profit of the state or pleasure of the rich? How many lands has it taken against the wills of the citizens of those lands? And the torture! It has burned alive human beings, ordered the tearing apart of humans by wild beasts in the hippodromes. This Satan is guilty of unimaginable thievery. This serpent has stolen the freedom of millions. It has stolen silver and gold from the temple in Jerusalem and from the homes and buildings of countless others around this third of the world. It has taken life itself from children, women, old people, and the sick who were forced into poverty and slavery by this Satan. This ancient serpent is evil! Evil given form and power by humans who walk the earth with hearts of stone, without love, without mercy. It is evil that eats away at its own life, physically and spiritually, until, like the great city Rome, it condemns itself to its own destruction.

It is the One who has power. The One has given the angel power to lock up this dragon, this beast that thinks itself invincible and eternal. Lock up the jailers who have locked up so many of the innocent, then sent them to their death. Lock up the judges who judge without justice or truth. Lock up the tax collectors who bleed life from the people. Lock up the proconsuls who are the dragon's priests and enforced the unjust laws. Lock up the senate of Rome which passed laws saying the emperor can kill anyone he wants as long as it is not a senator. Lock up the army. Lock them up for crimes against humanity, for the burning of homes, the torture of innocent people, the smashing of children's heads against walls, the rape of women and girls, the stealing of all they could carry, and all this without question as to what is right and just. It is power that is locked up, power that is predicated on the death of others.

It is not just the Roman empire that is thrown into the pit for a thousand years. It is all empires, all power that turns itself into evil. It is the empires of the ancient past and empires yet to come that are part of this ancient serpent who knows no remorse or repentance.

Here Ends the Sixth Act

Rev. 20:11–15

20:11 Then I saw a great white throne and the one who sat on it; the earth and the heaven fled from his presence, and no place was found for them.

20:12 And I saw the dead, great and small, standing before the throne, and books were opened. Also another book was opened, the book of life. And the dead were judged according to their works, as recorded in the books.

20:13 And the sea gave up the dead that were in it, Death and Hades gave up the dead that were in them, and all were judged according to what they had done.

20:14 Then Death and Hades were thrown into the lake of fire. This is the second death, the lake of fire;

20:15 and anyone whose name was not found written in the book of life was thrown into the lake of fire.

How Long, O Lord, How Long?

"Be ready!
Like a thief in the night,
Jesus is coming soon.
Jesus may come tomorrow.
Jesus may come today.
Jesus may come right now.
If we drop the bombs, He will come.

"I have it from God,
He is coming.
Go to the stadium,
Go to the mountain,
Go to the cave.
Believe my way,
We are special,
We are the 144,000."

"When will Jesus come?
We have waited.
We have gone to the stadium,
We have gone to the mountain,
We have gone to the cave.
When will Jesus come?
How long, O Lord, how long?"

"We don't hear an answer,
Because we ask the wrong question.
Not, how long before Jesus comes,
Rather, can we survive till he gets here?"

Act VII

Rev. 20:4–22:5

Rev. 20:4–10

20:4 Then I saw thrones, and those seated on them were given authority to judge. I also saw the souls of those who had been beheaded for their testimony to Jesus and for the word of God. They had not worshiped the beast or its image and had not received its mark on their foreheads or their hands. They came to life and reigned with Christ a thousand years.

20:5 (The rest of the dead did not come to life until the thousand years were ended.) This is the first resurrection.

20:6 Blessed and holy are those who share in the first resurrection. Over these the second death has no power, but they will be priests of God and of Christ, and they will reign with him a thousand years.

20:7 When the thousand years are ended, Satan will be released from his prison

20:8 and will come out to deceive the nations at the four corners of the earth, Gog and Magog, in order to gather them for battle; they are as numerous as the sands of the sea.

The Setting

How much longer will this play go on? We are fatigued of sitting, of thinking, of cheering, of jeering, of crying, of praying. We are fatigued by surprises, by war, by evil, and by death. We need a rest.

The One has taken pity on us and declared peace. In the beginning of this seventh act God declares a sabbath. There will be a thousand years on the earth when the power of empires and the evil they spawn will stay in the bottomless pit. At the beginning of this seventh act, our play has come to this sabbath rest. This sabbath will be one of God's days, for a thousand years in God's sight is but a day.

This is the last act. I am pleased you have stuck it out with me. The audience is sitting quietly as we watch the thrones of the twelve apostles and the twelve elders of Israel being carried onto the stage. Soon we are on our feet cheering as we recognize coming onto the stage those from our communities who have been beheaded. These are both the Christians who have been martyred for their testimony to Jesus and the Jews who had been faithful to the word of God. What a great day, this day of sabbath rest. Here on the stage before us are those whose souls have been held so long under the altar, calling out

> "How long, O Lord, how long?" "They have not worshiped the beast or its image and have not received its mark on their foreheads or their hands. They came to life and will reign with Christ a thousand years."

They would not give in to the state and give up their faith, even for the moment it took to burn a pinch of incense and say "Caesar is Lord." We are told "the second death has no power" over these martyred souls. The Jews will be priests

133

Rev. 20:9–10

20:9 They marched up over the breadth of the earth and surrounded the camp of the saints and the beloved city. And fire came down from heaven and consumed them.

20:10 And the devil who had deceived them was thrown into the lake of fire and sulfur, where the beast and the false prophet were, and they will be tormented day and night forever and ever.

of God and the Christians will be priests of Christ, and they will reign with him a thousand years.

A thousand years of justice, a thousand years of mercy, a thousand years of righteousness, a thousand years of peace, a thousand years of love, a thousand years of equality among humans, a thousand years of abundance for all people, that is what they will cause to happen. The Kingdom of God come upon the earth for a thousand years.

The audience starts stomping and booing when we are told that after this thousand years has ended, the red dragon, that is called Satan and the empire, will be released from his prison. How can the One let the evil soul of empire loose again upon the earth? It will go right back to its old tricks. It is the nature of empires to deceive the nations and call upon them for death. It has been the nature of empires since time began. It will remain their nature until this great sabbath day of the Lord comes upon the earth, and empires are thrown into the bottomless pit.

Even after a thousand years' imprisonment, the nature of empires will still be evil. After a thousand years Ezekiel's ancient evil empire Magog with its king Gog[1] will be called upon by the red dragon to wage war on the beloved city. They will surround the beloved city, as numerous as the sands of the sea, ready to destroy her, as we just saw the evil city of the empire destroy herself.

We start dancing in the aisles, as we watch the sun in the sky blow up and consume Gog and Magog.

"The devil, red dragon, empire, was thrown into the lake of fire and sulfur, where the beast and the false prophet were, and they will be tormented day and night forever and ever."

It is power, power over human beings by other human beings, that goes into the lake of fire with the red dragon.

---

[1] Ezekiel 38:17–39:8

Scene 1

We all hide our eyes from the great white throne that appears on the stage in this first scene of act seven. Seated on the throne is the One who has appeared in the setting of act two.

"And the One seated there looks like jasper and carnelian."[2]

We cannot stand to look at such a glorious sight. We are afraid that if we look at the great white throne we will die. Here is the true glory that the emperors have tried to steal for themselves. We can hide from the emperors. We can run into the darkness, into the caves, into safe houses scattered around the empire and be protected. Not so from the Great White Throne. There is no place we can go, there is no place we can look, there is no escaping the blinding splendor of that presence. The light penetrates to the marrow of our bones.

"The earth and the heaven fled from the presence, and no place was found for them."

Rev. 20:11

20:11 Then I saw a great white throne and the one who sat on it; the earth and the heaven fled from his presence, and no place was found for them.

---

[2] Revelation 4: 3

Rev. 20:12–15

20:12 And I saw the dead, great and small, standing before the throne, and books were opened. Also another book was opened, the book of life. And the dead were judged according to their works, as recorded in the books.

20:13 And the sea gave up the dead that were in it, Death and Hades gave up the dead that were in them, and all were judged according to what they had done.

20:14 Then Death and Hades were thrown into the lake of fire. This is the second death, the lake of fire;

20:15 and anyone whose name was not found written in the book of life was thrown into the lake of fire.

Scene 2

A multitude without number, including all the martyred, all the dead children, all the dead old ones, all the women and all the men passed before the throne. All that had died in the sea passed before the throne. Death gave up the Jews and Hades gave up the Christians and they all passed before the throne.

The books are opened: the books of the empire that have recorded the birth of every individual, and have kept track of who has offered the pinch of incense; the books of the dead that hold the names of those who have been martyred; and also another book is opened, the book of life. "The dead were judged according to their works as recorded in the books."

The audience begins to argue among themselves,

"So what we do does make a difference."

What a debate we have had over that one! The Jews kept the law and now we know it counts for their salvation. The Christians lived under grace,[3] but many of us follow the martyred James who said, "Faith without works is dead."[4] Some remind us of Paul, who taught that if inhabitants of the earth keep the law in their hearts, they are a law unto themselves.[5] Many in the audience cannot accept this and the great argument continues.

We stop our arguing when we see Death and Hades being thrown into the lake of fire. There is no more death, there is no more Hades! This lake of fire is the second death.

"Anyone whose name was not found written in the book of life was thrown into the lake of fire!"

So how did a person get left out of the book of life? It starts the argument all over again. What does a person have to do to get left out? Be born of non-believing parents? Renounce being a Christian or Jew? There are some who say no one is left out except the first beast emperor, the second beast proconsul-priest, and those who give the red dragon its power. They are the only ones we know for sure are thrown into the lake of fire.

---

[3] Romans 6: 14–15
[4] James 2: 17
[5] Romans 2: 14–17

Scene 3

Something we thought impossible for a play unfolds before us. There on the stage is a new heaven and a new earth. The first heaven and the first earth are burned up when the sun explodes and consumes the earth and burns Gog and Magog. It is this blast that is the lake of fire that burns the dragon-empire, the first beast-emperor, and the second beast-proconsul-priest. It is this explosion of the sun that destroys Death and Hades and dries up the sea, so it is no more. Can we count the days and months and years before the sun explodes, and there comes a new heaven and a new earth?

"How long, O Lord, how long?"

Rev. 21:1

21:1 Then I saw a new heaven and a new earth; for the first heaven and the first earth had passed away, and the sea was no more.

Rev. 21:2–8

21:2 And I saw the holy city, the new Jerusalem, coming down out of heaven from God, prepared as a bride adorned for her husband.

21:3 And I heard a loud voice from the throne saying, See, the home of God is among mortals. He will dwell with them as their God; they will be his peoples, and God himself will be with them;

21:4 he will wipe every tear from their eyes. Death will be no more; mourning and crying and pain will be no more, for the first things have passed away."

21:5 And the one who was seated on the throne said, "See, I am making all things new." Also he said, "Write this, for these words are trustworthy and true."

Scene 4

"And I saw the holy city, the new Jerusalem, coming down out of heaven from God, prepared as a bride adorned for her husband."

The audience is silent before the beauty of the Holy City. Its beauty far surpasses the city and temple that were burned by the Romans.

What a gift to those who are loved by the One. We are not forgotten by the One. Even in the midst of the empire's greatest evil, we are never forgotten. The One makes all things new, a new heaven and a new earth.

A loud voice from the throne said,

> "See, the home of God is among mortals.
> He will dwell with them as their God;
> They will be his peoples,
> And God himself will be with them;
> he will wipe every tear from their eyes.
> Death will be no more;
> mourning and crying and pain will be no more,
> for the first things have passed away."

On that day there will be no more tears, but there are countless tears in the audience now. We are weeping for the joy of knowing that the place of God is with us, and that evil will lose.

Then we hear the voice of the One seated on the throne proclaim,

> "See, I am making all things new. Write this, for these words are trustworthy and true. I am the Alpha and the Omega, the beginning and the end."

This is our Creator God who we thought had forgotten us in the days of our tribulation.

This is our Creator God who brought all things into being through the Word. This is our Creator God who will not forsake us or forget us because of the promise made to us. This is our Creator God who at the end of the first heaven and first earth now makes all things new. The One is the Alpha and Omega, the Beginning and the End.

Come, Lord Jesus, we thirst for life in your presence. Come, give life to those who conquer. Be our God and let us be your children.

"But as for the cowardly, the faithless, the polluted, (O My), the murderers, the fornicators, the sorcerers, (O Dear), the idolaters, and all liars, (O Me), their place will be in the lake that burns with fire and sulfur, which is the second death."

Now our tears are tears of fear, for who can escape the lake of fire? We are confused. In scene two, anyone who did not have their name written in the book of life would be thrown into that lake of fire. But remember how we did not know who that was, except the empire, the emperor, and the Roman state priests. We were not sure any other human being actually ended up there. Now we are all going. Who is not a coward, and who has not told lies? Does no one go, or do we all go to that lake of fire? A tax collector stands in the audience, beats his breast, and with his head bowed cries out, "God, have mercy on me, a sinner."[6]

Rev. 21:6–8

21:6 Then he said to me, "It is done! I am the Alpha and the Omega, the beginning and the end. To the thirsty I will give water as a gift from the spring of the water of life.

21:7 Those who conquer will inherit these things, and I will be their God and they will be my children.

21:8 But as for the cowardly, the faithless, the polluted, the murderers, the fornicators, the sorcerers, the idolaters, and all liars, their place will be in the lake that burns with fire and sulfur, which is the second death."

---

[6] Luke 18:13

Rev. 21:9–21

21:9   Then one of the seven angels who had the seven bowls full of the seven last plagues came and said to me, "Come, I will show you the bride, the wife of the Lamb."

21:10   And in the spirit he carried me away to a great, high mountain and showed me the holy city Jerusalem coming down out of heaven from God.

21:11   It has the glory of God and a radiance like a very rare jewel, like jasper, clear as crystal.

21:12   It has a great, high wall with twelve gates, and at the gates twelve angels, and on the gates are inscribed the names of the twelve tribes of the Israelites;

21:13   on the east three gates, on the north three gates, on the south three gates, and on the west three gates.

21:14   And the wall of the city has twelve foundations, and on them are the twelve names of the twelve apostles of the Lamb.

21:15   The angel who talked to me had a measuring rod of gold to measure the city and its gates and walls.

21:16   The city lies foursquare, its length the same as its width; and he measured the city with his rod, fifteen hundred miles; its length and width and height are equal.

21:17   He also measured its wall, one hundred forty-four cubits by human measurement, which the angel was using.

Scene 5

One of the seven angels who had the seven bowls full of the seven last plagues comes and says to John,

"Come, I will show you the bride, the wife of the Lamb."

And in the spirit he carries John away to a great, high mountain. Do you remember? We have seen this angel before. Earlier, in the setting for act six this angel carried John away in the spirit to the wilderness to show John,

"the judgment of the great whore who is seated on many waters, with whom the kings of the earth have committed fornication, and with the wine of whose fornication the inhabitants of the earth have become drunk."

After experiencing the corruption and evil of the great whore, how holy and pure this woman, this new Jerusalem, looks to us coming down out of heaven from God.

The new city

"has the glory of God and a radiance like a very rare jewel, like jasper, clear as crystal."

The audience is silent as they stare at her splendor. She has the very color and brilliance of God.

"It has a great, high wall with twelve gates, and at the gates twelve angels, and on the gates are inscribed the names of the twelve tribes of the Israelites; on the east three gates, on the north three gates, on the south three gates, and on the west three gates."

She will not be burned by the Romans or any empire yet to come. She will not have to be defended by brave but ill-trained Jews, as was the Jerusalem burned by the Romans: she is protected by her great high wall and the twelve angels of God. Unlike the cherubim God placed at the east of the garden of Eden with flaming sword to prevent humans from entering and finding the way to the tree of life,[7] these

---

[7] Genesis 3:24

angels are at the gates of this new Jerusalem to invite people in.

These angels stand at the twelve gates calling for all to enter. God has given the twelve gates of the New Jeruslam to the Jews for they have always shown the way. They have been lights to the nations. They have been God's chosen people to proclaim salvation to all who would hear. Now the angels are calling us, Jews and Christians and all the people of the earth who have a right to the tree of life, to enter the city by the tribes of the Jews, who are the gates. And this wall, so great and high, gets its strength from the faith of the twelve apostles of the Lamb who form its foundations.

We watch as the angel who took John to the high mountain measures her with a rod of gold.

"The city lies foursquare, its length the same as its width . . . and its length and width and height are equal."

The audience raise their hands in praise to realize the new city is a cube like the most Holy Place, the Holy of Holies of the burned temple.[8] This Holy Place, however, is not just for the High Priest; the angels stand at the gates calling for *all people* to enter. The wall is the color of God, and she is made of pure gold so fine it is clear as glass. Each foundation of the wall has its own color, from the same precious stones used in the ephod of the High Priest. Each gate is a pearl.

Rev. 21:18–21

21:18 The wall is built of jasper, while the city is pure gold, clear as glass.

21:19 The foundations of the wall of the city are adorned with every jewel; the first was jasper, the second sapphire, the third agate, the fourth emerald,

21:20 the fifth onyx, the sixth carnelian, the seventh chrysolite, the eighth beryl, the ninth topaz, the tenth chrysoprase, the eleventh jacinth, the twelfth amethyst.

21:21 And the twelve gates are twelve pearls, each of the gates is a single pearl, and the street of the city is pure gold, transparent as glass.

---

[8] I Kings 6:20

Rev. 21:22–27

21:22 I saw no temple in the city, for its temple is the Lord God the Almighty and the Lamb.

21:23 And the city has no need of sun or moon to shine on it, for the glory of God is its light, and its lamp is the Lamb.

21:24 The nations will walk by its light, and the kings of the earth will bring their glory into it.

21:25 Its gates will never be shut by day—and there will be no night there.

21:26 People will bring into it the glory and the honor of the nations.

21:27 But nothing unclean will enter it, nor anyone who practices abomination or falsehood, but only those who are written in the Lamb's book of life.

Scene 6

The audience begins asking each other where the temple is in this new City of God.

"There is no temple," someone yells out. "This city does not need a temple, for the city itself is the Holy of Holies. It is a cube like the Holy of Holies burned by the Romans. She is the very place where God dwells, like the Holy of Holies Moses entered in the wilderness to talk with God face to face."

"Then is this city only for the Jews?" *someone asks.*

A woman answers,

"Not just for the Jews, for now the Lamb of God is present."

"The nations will walk by its light, and the kings of the earth will bring their glory into it. . . . People will bring into it the glory and the honor of the nations."

So you see my friend the new City of God will be the home of all the nations, of all the people, of all tribes and tongues, of all kings and rulers. I pray, my friend, it will be our home as well.

The sun has exploded, and the old heaven and the old earth are gone. From where does the light come?
The angel proclaimed,

"And the city has no need of sun or moon to shine on it, for the glory of God is its light, and its lamp is the Lamb."

There will never be night there, and the gates of pearl, one for each of the tribes of Israel, will never roll shut, for there are no enemies of the city of God. The One has redeemed all the earth.

"Nothing unclean will enter,"

for the One has redeemed, and will continue to redeem all people, for only the name redeemed is written in the Lamb's book of life.

Scene 7

There is a river on the stage.

"This river had the water of life, bright as crystal, flowing from the throne of God and of the Lamb through the middle of the street of the city."

"That's the river of life that flows out of the Garden of Eden,"[9] *someone yells.* "That water will give life to all of paradise!"

"On either side of the river is the tree of life with its twelve kinds of fruit, producing its fruit each month; and the leaves of the tree are for the healing of the nations."

Someone shouts, "This is the new temple of God,"

Like the fig tree withered by the Lamb, the old temple did not give fruit.[10] Now this temple gives twelve kinds of fruit, one for each month. The old temple had to be served by one of the twelve tribes each month. We do not have to serve this temple; it serves us and bears a different kind of fruit for all the people. The old temple was a house of prayer for all nations,[11] and now the leaves of this tree of life in the middle of the new temple will be for the healing of all the nations. There will be no more accursed or unclean nations for they have all been healed, and there can be nothing accursed or unclean found in this new City of God. Never again will the temple of the One be filled with blood and death as it was by the Romans. But the throne of God and of the Lamb will be in the new temple, the New City. The Jews, God's servants, will worship the One; they will, like Moses, see God's face. The name of the One will be on their foreheads, put there as a seal in scene six of act two. The Christians will be present with the Lamb of God in the new city of God. The home for all who will believe.

"And there will be no more night; they will need no light of lamp or sun, for the Lord God will be their light, and they will reign forever and ever."

Here Ends the Seventh Act

---

[9] Genesis 2:10
[10] Mark 11:20–26
[11] Isaiah 56:6–8

22:1 Then the angel showed me the river of the water of life, bright as crystal, flowing from the throne of God and of the Lamb

22:2 through the middle of the street of the city. On either side of the river is the tree of life with its twelve kinds of fruit, producing its fruit each month; and the leaves of the tree are for the healing of the nations.

22:3 Nothing accursed will be found there any more. But the throne of God and of the Lamb will be in it, and his servants will worship him;

22:4 they will see his face, and his name will be on their foreheads.

22:5 And there will be no more night; they need no light of lamp or sun, for the Lord God will be their light, and they will reign forever and ever.

Epilogue

Rev. 22:6–20

22:6 And he said to me, "These words are trustworthy and true, for the Lord, the God of the spirits of the prophets, has sent his angel to show his servants what must soon take place."

22:7 "See, I am coming soon! Blessed is the one who keeps the words of the prophecy of this book."

22:8 I, John, am the one who heard and saw these things. And when I heard and saw them, I fell down to worship at the feet of the angel who showed them to me;

22:9 but he said to me, "You must not do that! I am a fellow servant with you and your comrades the prophets, and with those who keep the words of this book. Worship God!"

22:10 And he said to me, "Do not seal up the words of the prophecy of this book, for the time is near.

22:11 Let the evildoer still do evil, and the filthy still be filthy, and the righteous still do right, and the holy still be holy."

22:12 "See, I am coming soon; my reward is with me, to repay according to everyone's work.

The angel says to John,

"These words are trustworthy and true, for the Lord, and the God of the spirits of the prophets, has sent his angel to show his servants what must soon take place."

We all know that the God of the spirits of the prophets is the God of the Jews. The Jews in the audience are happy that the rest of us now see they have not been left out of the One's plan of redemption, but we all are included in the new City of God.

The angel speaks the words of Christ and says,

"See, I am coming soon! Blessed is the one who keeps the words of the prophecy of this book."

The audience calls back,

"How long, O Lord, how long!"

John faces the audience and says,

"I, John, am the one who heard and saw these things. And when I heard and saw them, I fell down to worship at the feet of the angel who showed them to me; but he said to me, 'You must not do that! I am a fellow servant with you and your comrades the prophets, and with those who keep the words of this book. Worship God!'"

The angel tells John,

"Do not seal up the words of the prophecy of this book, for the time is near. Let the evildoer still do evil, and the filthy still be filthy, and the righteous still do right, and the holy still be holy."

"Yes," we yell, "Life goes on. How long, O Lord, how long?"

The voice of the One says,

"See, I am coming soon; my reward is with me, to repay according to everyone's work. I am the Alpha and the Omega, the first and the last, the beginning and the end."

"We will receive according to our work. Then who can stand?"

Someone shouted,

"We are sinners, (O My), we are doubters, (O Dear), we are lost (O Me)," and then we hear again the voice of the tax collector who is beating his breast and saying,

"God be merciful to me, a sinner.'"

John says,

"Blessed are those who wash their robes, so that they will have the right to the tree of life and may enter the city by the gates."

We think of all those who have died at the hands of the Romans, those who have died in the Holy City, those who have died in slavery. We think of those who have died because they were Christian, those who have died of poverty created by the empire. We think of those who are dead, who are dying, those who will yet die at the hands of empires. These are the ones who have washed their robes in the blood of the Lamb, the blood shed by the empire. They will have the right to the tree of life and may enter the city by the gates.

There are still those outside the city: the dogs, the sorcerers, fornicators and murderers and idolaters, and everyone who loves and practices falsehood. Standing at the gates of the city, we see the Spirit of the One who, together with the City herself, yells to the dogs, the sorcerers, fornicators and murderers and idolaters, and everyone who loves and practices falsehood,

"Come."
    "And let everyone who hears say, 'Come.' And let everyone who is thirsty come. Let anyone who wishes take the water of life as a gift."

Rev. 22:13–17

22:13 I am the Alpha and the Omega, the first and the last, the beginning and the end."

22:14 Blessed are those who wash their robes, so that they will have the right to the tree of life and may enter the city by the gates.

22:15 Outside are the dogs and sorcerers and fornicators and murderers and idolaters, and everyone who loves and practices falsehood.

22:16 "It is I, Jesus, who sent my angel to you with this testimony for the churches. I am the root and the descendant of David, the bright morning star."

22:17 The Spirit and the bride say, "Come." And let everyone who hears say, "Come." And let everyone who is thirsty come. Let anyone who wishes take the water of life as a gift.

Rev. 22:18–20

22:18 I warn everyone who hears the words of the prophecy of this book: if anyone adds to them, God will add to that person the plagues described in this book;

22:19 if anyone takes away from the words of the book of this prophecy, God will take away that person's share in the tree of life and in the holy city, which are described in this book.

22:20 The one who testifies to these things says, "Surely I am coming soon." Amen. Come, Lord Jesus!

Even in the New Jerusalem, even in the new City of God, the One is not finished with redeeming us. The One will never stop yelling, "Come," as long as there is one soul outside the city. The One will never stop redeeming as long as one soul is in pain or separation. The One will never give up on a human being as long as he or she will hear the call, "Come, drink the water that gives life!"

There on the stage is one like a Lamb that has been slaughtered. He says,

"It is I, Jesus, who sent my angel to you with this testimony for the churches. I am the root and the descendant of David,[1] the bright morning star."[2]

The audience cheers, for we know this testimony is not just for the churches. It is for both Christians and Jews, as it has come from the one who is the descendant of David.

The One who has been slaughtered continues,

"I warn everyone who hears the words of the prophecy of this book: If anyone adds to them, God will add to that person the plagues described in this book; if anyone takes away from the words of the book of this prophecy, God will take away that person's share in the tree of life and in the holy city, which are described in this book."

"O God be merciful to me, a sinner!"

"The One who testifies to these things says, 'Surely I am coming soon.'"
"How long, O Lord, how long?'"
"Amen. Come, Lord Jesus!"

Closing Benediction
I hope, my friend the reader, you have found this play a blessing. As we leave silently from the theater we hear the voice of the angel, "The grace of the Lord Jesus be with all the saints. Amen."

Did you find the third woe?
The One has not finished redeeming us!

---

[1] Isaiah 11:1, 10
[2] Revelation 2:28

Notes

1. After the fire in Rome, A.D. 64:
"But all human efforts, all the lavish gifts of the emperor, and the propitiations of the gods, did not banish the sinister belief that the conflagration was the result of an order. Consequently, to get rid of the report, Nero fastened the guilt and inflicted the most exquisite tortures on a class hated for their abominations, called Christians by the populace. Christus, from whom the name had its origin, suffered the extreme penalty during the reign of Tiberius at the hands of one of our procurators, Pontius Pilatus, and a most mischievous superstition, thus checked for the moment, again broke out not only in Judea, the first source of the evil, but even in Rome, where all things hideous and shameful from every part of the world find their center and become popular. Accordingly, an arrest was first made of all who pleaded guilty; then, upon their information, an immense multitude was convicted, not so much of the crime of firing the city, as of hatred against mankind. Mockery of every sort was added to their deaths. Covered with the skins of beasts, they were torn by dogs and perished, or were nailed to crosses, or were doomed to the flames and burnt, to serve as a nightly illumination when daylight had expired.

Nero offered his gardens for the spectacle, and was exhibiting a show in the circus, while he mingled with the people in the dress of a charioteer or stood aloft on a car. Hence, even for criminals who deserved extreme and exemplary punishment, there arose a feeling of compassion; for it was not, as it seemed, for the public good, but to glut one man's cruelty, that they were being destroyed."

Reprinted by permission from *Encyclopaedia Britannica*, 1952, 1990. "Great Books Of The Western World," p. 168. "The Annals, Book XV44 Tactitus"

After the burning of Jerusalem including the temple, A.D. 70:
"Tacitus in his *History* says that the population of Jerusalem at the beginning of the siege [of Jerusalem], was about six hundred thousand. Josephus says that during the five months of the siege eleven hundred thousand died; but this figure includes the pilgrims who had crowded into Jerusalem for Passover in the spring and could not get out. Josephus' figure apparently also includes the Jews killed in the mopping-up operation after the city had fallen. The soldiers got rid of any aged and infirm people still in existence, although Titus had specified that only people carrying weapons should die. Both Tacitus' and Josephus' estimates are probably much exaggerated, but the toll must still have been tremendous.

As for the prisoners, they were herded into the ruins of the Temple, where a friend of Titus divided them into various categories. Those who had been agitators were executed. The best-looking young men were saved for the triumph that Titus expected to stage at Rome. The rest were sent in chains to Egypt to labor in the mines, sold as slaves (if they were young enough to have a future), or distributed to various provinces of the empire, if they were strong enough to be used in gladiatorial combats or pitted against beasts in the arena."

Reprinted by permission from *Judaea Weeping: The Jewish Struggle Against Rome from Pompey to Masada, 63 B.C. to 73 A.D.*, George C. Brauer, Jr., (Thomas Y. Crowell Company, New York, New York. 1970) p. 262.

2. Ships of the Empire:
"The most important crops of the Empire were wheat (especially in Egypt, which supplied the city of Rome), grapes, olives (for oil), and vegetables. Papyrus also came from Egypt. Mining, both open-cut and underground, was carried on for gold, silver, lead, tin, copper, and iron. Most of the mines belonged to the state and were worked by slaves. Marble was quarried chiefly in Greece, though some use was also made of the Italian stone. Manufacturing in pottery, textiles, leather, metals, and glass was the work chiefly of slaves and freedmen, sometimes associated in syndicates which provided capital and banking facilities for the various branches of the business. Agricultural and manufactured goods were transported either overland on the excellent Roman road system (stone and concrete) or through the Mediterranean and other seas by ship. Highwaymen continued to present difficulties, but at sea the pirates had been exterminated, and Roman patrol vessels safeguarded both the Mediterranean and the west coast of Europe. In the early Empire 120 vessels a year sailed to India, exporting linen, coral, glass, and metals, and importing perfumes, spices, gems, ivory, pearls, and Chinese silk."

Reprinted by permission from *The Interpreter's Dictionary of the Bible* , Vol. 4 (Nashville: Abingdon Press, 1962) p. 105.

After the destruction of Jerusalem:
"Titus now proceeded on his intended journey to Egypt; crossing the desert as quickly as possible, he reached Alexandria. . . . The leaders of the captives, Simon and John, together with the seven hundred men he had picked as being eminently tall and handsome in body, he ordered to be immediately transported to Italy, wishing to exhibit them at the triumph."

Reprinted by permission from *Jerusalem and Rome: The Writings of Josephus* (War VII, 5: 1–3), selected and introduced by Nahum N. Glatzer (Meridian Books, New York City) p. 277.

3. Water of Bitterness:
"A husband who suspected his wife of infidelity, but had no legal proof, could bring her to the sanctuary, where, under conditions calculated to terrify the guilty, her innocence was tested. She was seated before the sanctuary facing the altar (in later times at the east gate of the temple; M. Sot. 1.5), where she would be exposed directly to Yahweh's power of blessing and cursing. Her hair was unbound as a sign of her shame, and, according to the Mishna, she was clothed in black and had her bosom bare (Sot. 115–6). The priest placed in her hands her husband's cereal offering, called an "offering of remembrance;" took dust from the floor of the sanctuary to enhance the sacredness of the potion; placed it in "holy water" (LXX "living," i.e., running water); and, standing before the woman, pronounced a terrible curse, with which she irrevocably identified herself by a double "amen." The words of a written copy of the curse were washed into the water, the cereal offering made, and the woman compelled to drink. If she was guilty, the lower part of her body became distorted; if innocent, she was unharmed and received the blessing of bearing children."

Reprinted by permission from *The Interpreter's Dictionary Of The Bible,* Vol. 4, (Nashville: Abingdon Press,1962) p. 811 and Numbers 5:11ff.

4. Nero as the Sun God:
"His effigy of Nero, which stood between 110 and 120 feet high, was erected as the centre-piece for the vestibule of the palace where it probably stood within a central

colonnaded court overlooking the forum. The emperor's brow was crowned with rays suggesting a comparison or identification with the sun-god."

Reprinted by permission from *Nero: Emperor in Revolt*, Michael Grant (New York: American Heritage Publishing, 1970). p. 178

5. Nero Among the Stars:
"The image of Nero driving a chariot and surrounded by golden stars on the awning over the theater where Tiridates received his crown is interpreted as a representation of the emperor as the incarnation of Mithras, a deity closely associated with the sun."

Reprinted by permission from *Nero, The End of a Dynasty*, Griffin (New Haven, CT: Yale University Press, 1984).

6. Armies as Locusts in the Old Testament:
"What the cutting locust left, the swarming locust has eaten. What the swarming locust left, the hopping locust has eaten, and what the hopping locust left, the destroying locust has eaten. Wake up, you drunkards, and weep; and wail all you wine-drinkers, over the sweet wine, for it is cut off from your mouth. For a nation has invaded my land, powerful and innumerable; its teeth are lion's teeth, and it has the fangs of a lioness. . . . Blow the trumpet in Zion; sound the alarm on my holy mountain! Let all the inhabitants of the land tremble, for the day of the Lord is coming, it is near—a day of darkness and gloom, a day of clouds and thick darkness! Like blackness spread upon the mountains a great and powerful army comes; their like has never been from of old, nor will be again after them in ages to come." Joel 1: 4–43 and 2: 1–2.

7. A description of how the Proconsul Pliny acted as Proconsul, Priest, and Judge of the Christians. This is a letter from Proconsul Pliny to the emperor Trajan:
Pliny, to the Emperor Trajan:

It is my custom to refer all my difficulties to you, Sir, for no one is better able to resolve my doubts and to inform my ignorance.

I have never been present at an examination of Christians. Consequently, I do not know the nature or the extent of the punishments usually meted out to them, nor the grounds for starting an investigation and how far it should be pressed. Nor am I at all sure whether any distinction should be made between them on the grounds of age, or if young people and adults should be treated alike; whether a pardon ought to be granted to anyone retracting his beliefs, or if he has once professed Christianity, he shall gain nothing by renouncing it; and whether it is the mere name of Christian which is punishable, even if innocent of crime, or rather the crimes associated with the name.

For the moment this is the line I have taken with all persons brought before me on the charge of being Christians. I have asked them in person if they are Christians, and if they admit it, I repeat the question a second and third time, with a warning of the punishment awaiting them. If they persist, I order them to be led away for execution; for, whatever the nature of their admission, I am convinced that their stubbornness and unshakeable obstinacy ought not to go unpunished. There have been others similarly fanatical who are Roman citizens. I have entered them on the list of persons to be sent to Rome for trial.

Now that I have begun to deal with this problem, as so often happens, the charges are becoming more widespread and increasing in variety. An anonymous pamphlet has been circulated which contains the names of a number of accused persons.

Among these I considered that I should dismiss any who denied that they were or ever had been Christians when they had repeated after me a formula of invocation to the gods and had made offerings of wine and incense to your statue (which I had ordered to be brought into court for this purpose along with the images of the gods), and furthermore had reviled the name of Christ; none of which things, I understand, any genuine Christian can be induced to do.

Others, whose names were given to me by an informer, first admitted the charge and then denied it; they said that they had ceased to be Christians two or more years previously, and some of them even twenty years ago. They all did reverence to your statue and the images of the gods in the same way as the others, and reviled the name of Christ. They also declared that the sum total of their guilt or error amounted to no more than this; they had met regularly before dawn on a fixed day to chant verses alternately among themselves in honor of Christ as if to a god, and also to bind themselves by oath, not for any criminal purpose, but to abstain from theft, robbery and adultery, to commit no breach of trust and not to deny a deposit when called upon to restore it. After this ceremony it had been their custom to disperse and reassemble later to take food of an ordinary, harmless kind; but they had in fact given up this practice since my edict, issued on your instructions, which banned all political societies. This made me decide it was all the more necessary to extract the truth by torture from two slave-women, whom they call deaconesses. I found nothing but a degenerate sort of cult carried to extravagant lengths.

I have therefore postponed any further examination and hastened to consult you. The question seems to me to be worthy of your consideration, especially in view of the number of persons endangered; for a great many individuals of every age and class, both men and women, are being brought to trial, and this is likely to continue.

It is not only the towns, but villages and rural districts too which are infected through contact with this wretched cult. I think, though, that it is still possible for it to be checked and directed to better ends, for there is no doubt that people have begun to throng the temples which had been almost entirely deserted for a long time; the sacred rites which had been allowed to lapse are being performed again, and flesh of sacrificial victims is on sale everywhere, though up till recently scarcely anyone could be found to buy it. It is easy to infer from this that a great many people could be reformed if they were given an opportunity to repent.

XCVII, Trajan to Pliny:
You have followed the right course of procedure, my dear Pliny, in your examination of the cases of persons charged with being Christians, for it is impossible to lay down a general rule to a fixed formula. These people must not be hunted out; if they are brought before you and the charge against them is proved, they must be punished, but in the case of anyone who denies that he is a Christian, and makes it clear that he is not by offering prayers to our gods, he is to be pardoned as a result of his repentance, however suspect his past conduct may be. But pamphlets circulated anonymously must play no part in any accusation. They create the worst sort of precedent and are quite out of keeping with the spirit of our age.

Reprinted by permission from *Pliny: Letters and Panegyricus,* Vol. II, translated by Betty Radice (Cambridge, Massachusetts: Harvard University Press, 1969) p. 12 of Introduction: Pliny the Younger, "sent by Trajan as the Emperor's special representative to the province of Bithynia-Pontus."

Tom Jones earned his B.A. from Central Michigan University and M.Th. from Perkins School of Theology at Southern Methodist University. After serving seven years as parish pastor, Tom served as United Methodist Campus Pastor to the Central Michigan Community for fourteen years. He now serves a parish part time, writes, and he and his wife Ruth work a small farm in Central Michigan.